THE JOY OF WORKING FROM HOME

"Sometimes the answers we seek for the many problems of modern life are right in front of us. Jeff Berner teaches us a simple, direct route to greater personal fulfillment: how to receive more by doing less. It's our life. Jeff instructs us on how to spend it wisely."

Paul Hawken
Co-founder and former President, Smith & Hawken
Author, *The Ecology of Commerce, Growing a Business,* and *The Next Economy*

THE JOY OF WORKING FROM HOME

❖

MAKING A LIFE WHILE MAKING A LIVING

JEFF BERNER

Berrett-Koehler Publishers, Inc.
155 Montgomery Street
San Francisco, CA 94104-4109
Tel: 415-288-0260 Fax: 415-362-2512

ORDERING INFORMATION

Individual sales. Berrett-Koehler publications are available through most bookstores. They can also be ordered direct from Berrett-Koehler at the address above.

Quantity sales. Special discounts are available on quantity purchases by corporations, associations, and others. For details, contact the "Special Sales Department" at the Berrett-Koehler address above.

Orders for college textbook/course adoption use. Please contact Berrett-Koehler Publishers at the address above.

Orders by U.S. trade bookstores and wholesalers. Please contact Publishers Group West, 4065 Hollis Street, Box 8843, Emeryville, CA 94662; 510-658-3453; 1-800-788-3123.

Printed in the United States of America

Printed on acid-free and recycled paper that meets the strictest state and U.S. guidelines for recycled paper (50 percent recycled waste, including 10 percent postconsumer waste).

Library of Congress Cataloging-in-Publication Data

Berner, Jeff
The joy of working from home: making a life while making a living/ Jeff Berner

p. cm.
Includes bibliographical references and index.
ISBN 1-881052-46-X (paperback: Alk. paper)
1. Home-based businesses — Management. 2. Self-employed. 3. Telecommuting.
I. Title
HD62.38.B47 1994
658'.041—dc20 93-19624
CIP

First Edition
99 98 97 96 95 94 10 9 8 7 6 5 4 3 2 1

For my parents, Bill and Jeannette Berner, whose abiding love for learning instilled in me the courage to live creatively and work independently—in the spirit of community.

CONTENTS

Preface

It's Monday afternoon and I'm writing this in my home office, which overlooks the Pacific Ocean. This morning I made some phone calls, wrote five business letters, and finished a proposal for the next book I'm going to write. Soon I'll walk down the hill to my mailbox and pick up today's correspondence. I'll take a mid-afternoon break with a friend to go bicycling in the countryside and probably wrap up the workday answering phone messages and watering the lawn while most of my peers are creeping along the freeway. My own commute is about ten seconds—from the breakfast table, across the living room, to my desk in the office with the big picture window. I look forward to "going to work" almost every day.

Observing the life of salaried men in gray suits during my twenties, I chose a different path. During the subsequent thirty years, I have had the pleasure of balancing my personal and professional life as a writer, photographer, and marketing consultant serving clients in the United States, Canada, Great Britain, and the Far East—all while working from my home. I can work until three in the morning while the full moon shines over the water outside my office window or, if the mood strikes, I can go wine tasting in Napa Valley in the middle of a weekday afternoon. I have the luxury of taking on the projects I really want and of working with people I actually like. I can take breaks and vacations without applying for a hall pass. And I've never been fired. Whatever other struggles and victories have come my way, I have been sustained by the joy of not living under the thumb of a boss or at the mercy of fluctuating corporate fortunes.

Back in the late sixties, working at home was not considered very professional. However, it has become a much-envied lifestyle in the nineties. Friends and associates who in 1968 wondered why I didn't have a "real" office are now asking me how they can improve the quality of their lives by setting up home offices of their own.

I've learned a lot about running a small business and about being my own boss, and I continue to learn from members of the home-office workshops I conduct and from many colleagues who are on the same delightful path. My experience and that of my friends and colleagues has convinced me that, given a chance to blossom, each of us has a natural talent that can make a real contribution to the community while earning a living for ourselves and our families.

Five years ago, I was having lunch at a Silicon Valley restaurant when a corporate communications manager asked me where my office was. "In my home," I replied. Immediately, he appeared skeptical. He obviously thought that anyone working from home was only playing at a career or couldn't afford a "real" office. On the way home, I decided to write this book for everyone whose life has shrunk to the size of their job.

My hope is that you'll find the inspiration in these pages to take charge of your life and to make the most of your abilities. I have included as much information as possible to help you shape a successful life—either as a telecommuting team member in the corporate culture or as an independent professional. The most important thing for you to do is enjoy the adventure.

Jeff Berner
Marin County, California
Summer, 1994

p.s. If someone cheerfully says, "Have a good weekend!" and it's only Wednesday, you know they are probably working from home!

Acknowledgments

The author wishes to express heartfelt appreciation for the valuable editorial support and personal encouragement given by Steven Piersanti, editor-in-chief of Berrett-Koehler Publishers. He and his associates at Berrett-Koehler have created a publishing venture of which most authors only dream. Wanda Hale and longtime friend Cummings Walker, of Walker & Hale, Palo Alto, California, created the design for this book, adding an extra measure of vitality and pleasure to reading and learning. The author also wishes to thank Gary Schweikhart, public relations manager of Office Depot, Inc., who first recognized the need for a publication supporting the home-based worker's quest toward "making a life while making a living" and published the premium booklet version of this book. Thanks to Jennifer Myers, Jackie Taub, and Neva Beach for their preliminary critiques of the first draft. Independent writer and editor Elaine de Man has provided insightful editorial support, for which I am grateful. Thanks to Mali Apple and Cathy Steinberg for helping to fine-tune the final text, and to Bob Bergtholdt and Dean Ritz for cheering me on.

INTRODUCTION *The Trend Toward Working from Home*

A little more than one hundred years ago, nearly 90 percent of all Americans were self-employed and many worked from their homes. Doctors saw patients in their living rooms. Salesmen worked out of inventory in their garages or empty sheds. The grocer lived with his family upstairs above the store. Today, it's just the reverse: fewer than 9 percent of us are self-employed.

There are more people in America working from home—part time or full time—than the entire population of California.

Recently, however, the relative security of a salaried job with a good company has given way to a chronic sense of insecurity as jobs and companies that once inspired our loyalty disappear. Corporations are rushing to "downsize" and "rightsize" themselves, and skilled, educated people who had what they thought were lifetime careers are getting laid off and finding themselves at loose ends with no place to go. Not only are they losing their jobs, they are losing their medical benefits and, in some cases, their retirement packages. Most analysts believe that many jobs currently being eliminated in the corporate and governmental sectors are not likely to return. And, even if the job itself is secure, indebtedness and a deep sense of "time poverty" cuts across all professional levels. After commuting to work, working, and then commuting home again, there's almost no time left to do anything but eat, "relax" in front of the TV, and hope to sleep well enough to do it all over again. I certainly don't envy the average American worker today.

But during the past five years, an interesting thing has happened in living rooms, dining rooms, and bedrooms all across the nation. Millions of people have set up home offices and are working from their homes. Some chose to remain in the salaried culture and use their home office to catch up on corporate "homework." Others telecommute from their home office by sending their work in to their corporate headquarters from a personal computer via phone lines. (In fact, telecommuting suddenly became the "in thing" within hours of the January 1994 Los Angeles earthquake, which destroyed many of that sprawling city's freeways.) And many others swapped the insecurity of dependence on a corporation and the good will of a boss by starting their own home-based businesses—a new version of traditional American entrepreneurship and independence. They have wiped out the commute to and through congested urban areas and have saved their lifestyles and, perhaps, their lives.

There are 12 million full-time self-employed home workers, and an equal number of part-time self-employed people working from home, plus about nine million workers who take office work home with them. There are also about 7.5 million salaried people who use telecommunications to stay in touch with their companies.

From a Link Resources Corp. 1994 report

The trend toward working from home is encouraged not only by cultural change but by a rapidly evolving technology that is much more accessible and affordable than ever. A one- or two-person office can appear to the outside world like a fully staffed corporate warren, complete with fax machines, computers, and copiers. Equipped with a laptop computer and built-in fax/modem, you can carry this fully informed "office" onto a boat, into a hotel, or to the top of a mountain.

If you are currently in a salaried position, setting up a personal office now will give you a "lifeboat" to jump into if you suddenly become "job free," or the launching pad for a successful new business that puts *you* in charge. Ironically, as corporations shrink, they are relying more and more upon outside, independent suppliers and consultants who they don't have to cover with medical insurance and retirement plans. This means that the opportunities for independent professionals and tradespeople will get better even as the job market shrinks.

The transition to relative or total independence is no hop-skip-jump, however. Dagwood Bumstead of Sunday comics fame found this out the hard way in 1993 when he quit the job he'd held for sixty years working for Mr. Dithers and went to work with Blondie in her home-based catering business. Unfortunately, he literally ate all the profits and was summarily fired. Dagwood is now back at work for Mr. Dithers. But you, possessing more initiative and capable of more forethought than a two-dimensional comic character, will surely succeed.

Anyone who takes the plunge into telecommuting for a corporation or into working for herself, himself, or a small team of themselves is in for the ride of their lives. But whether that ride is a roller coaster or merry-go-round depends on you. By considering a few basics in advance and taking advantage of some time-proven rules of thumb, making a living from your home can become a liberating and profitable way to pay for the things in life that really count.

1

Succeeding in a New Life

Ten years ago, Robert Ortalda, a tax consultant and financial planner, abandoned his work with a small group practice in downtown San Francisco and established a personal office at home. Since he no longer had to pay for an expensive office, parking, and a two-hour round-trip commute, he could afford a charming, Spanish-style home in the suburbs. Mary, his wife, left her one-hour commute to a job as a technical supervisor for a general-ledger service bureau to join Robert as a part-time receptionist and bookkeeper. Not only does Robert save by not hiring outside help, he and Mary also have a lot more time together and with their children. They are reaping other financial rewards as well. For example, their home office allows them to take tax deductions for water, electricity, garbage collection, home repair, house cleaning, and gardening expenses.

Robert and Mary enjoy having their two young children at home most of the time, with just enough day care and babysitters to give everyone a break. They are learning about and from one another, and they are giving their children the opportunity to see how the family living is really made. The value of a dollar and the effort that earns it are more real. And perhaps most important, they know where their kids are, and the kids know where their parents are.

The Ortaldas did face a period of adjustment, however. Robert and Mary were both accustomed to the corporate office world, seeing each other mostly in the evening and on weekends. Once they began working together, they discovered differences in their working styles. Mary wanted to start the workday mid-morning; Robert was more interested in jump-starting the day at first light and calling it quits in the early afternoon, while Mary was still buzzing into early evening. Rather than letting this conflict spoil their new way of life, they devised an elegant solution: Robert started cooking more often, allowing Mary to wind down from her work and turn her attention to getting the children ready for dinner and bed. The Ortaldas have built something besides a bank account: a balanced business and family life.

Bob Oldfield, a long-time surfer and sailor, used to sell sailboats and wait tables to support his lifestyle. While his friends were hard at work, he spent long afternoons riding the curls in California and Hawaii and weeks at a time sailing in ocean-going races.

When he turned thirty-seven, the California bachelor started looking around for a way to increase his income. He was interested in marriage and wanted to develop some savings for future security. Since most career-change counselors recommend doing what you love, the obvious choice for Bob was to set up a business chartering and sailing boats for clients who wanted to spend a few days or weeks on the ocean. But Bob looked around at other avid sailors who had reduced their sport to a business laden with responsibility and liability, and decided that doing so would take the joy out of what he had been doing for self-discipline and bliss all his life. So he joined a small brokerage firm and began selling reconditioned computer workstations instead.

After a couple of years commuting and spending all day on the phone working for a boss who frequently appropriated leads that Bob had developed, he went out on his own. He set himself up in a small studio apartment just sixty feet from a delightful lagoon and a three-mile-long waterway where he keeps his thirteen-foot Laser sailboat. With a phone, an ancient answering machine, a fax machine, a couch, a pen, and a handful of index cards, Bob built his annual gross sales to six million dollars in seven years. He is supported in his venture by a partner seventy miles away who manages contract details on a computer, communicating with Bob via fax and phone.

Because Bob's business is global, he is on the phone many hours a day, often in the middle of the night. But he still has time for daily weight training, meditation, surfing along the coast with his girlfriend, and lots of ocean sailing.

In 1988 Robin Williams, then thirty-two years old and the mother of three small children, was living in a rented cottage with two closets and no garage or backyard. She was working part-time for a veterinarian and at other little jobs to support her family, and she received modest checks from the state welfare service. Her total income was eleven thousand dollars a year. Spurred by a desire to design her own books, she enrolled in a two-year program in graphic design and desktop publishing at a local junior college.

In 1989 Robin's father died, and she asked her mother to loan her some of the insurance money to buy a house. Her mother thought the idea was too risky, so Robin asked instead for a loan of fifteen thousand dollars so she could publish two little computer books she had written and designed. "And," she promised her mother, "I'll buy my own house in a year."

Money in hand, Robin produced both books and got them reviewed in national computer magazines, which raved about her unique style. Bookstores started asking for them, sales took off, and in just over a year she had sold five thousand copies of *The Little Mac Book* and three thousand copies of *The Mac Is Not a Typewriter.* The rights were picked up by Peachpit Press (Berkeley, California), who has since sold more than three hundred thousand copies of *The Little Mac Book*. The book has been translated into seven languages and, along with *The Mac Is Not a Typewriter,* is consistently one of the top ten bestselling books about the Macintosh in the world. In 1992 Robin took her three children, her mother, her two brothers and their wives, her sister and her sister's husband, plus two of her best friends on a week-long cruise to the Caribbean to thank them for being so supportive while she was struggling. She recently moved from the San Francisco Bay area to Santa Fe, where she bought a house just a little behind schedule. And all the while she was still a full-time mother to her three children.

For the Ortaldas, working from home improved family life and let them invest in home ownership. For Bob Oldfield, it meant multiplying his income without giving up his laid-back lifestyle. But for Robin Williams, a home office allowed her to remain a full-time mom while gaining financial independence and success with a platform from which she became truly independent.

It's not only young professionals and tradespeople who are setting up home offices. About half a million retirees are currently finding that home-based businesses are a graceful way to remain part of the action and keep their skills honed without having to take directions from managers half their age. The extra income adds to the quality of their lives, and being in business keeps the more experienced among us actively contributing to the community.

Are You Ready to Work from Home?

Management consultants, career counselors, corporate outplacement specialists, and psychologists are all busy churning out lists of traits required of people who work from their homes. Looking back on nearly three decades of my own home-based career, and seeing how my friends and colleagues are faring, I have no doubt that self-discipline, the ability to get and stay organized, goal-orientation, and self-confidence top the list, followed by decisiveness and, if you are working for yourself, an interest in profit.

Thousands of successful home office professionals and tradespeople are strong in some of these traits, but are weak in others. Consider these various components of success, and see how many you can bring to the desk. Be easy on yourself, but also try to be honest.

Self-discipline is absolutely essential, especially where food, drink, and other distractions are concerned. It is as important in dealing with laziness as it is in conquering workaholism—the twin demons that live in most home offices. I sometimes talk to myself with the voice of an imagined shareholder. First thing in the morning, I might look into the mirror and say to myself, "It's show time, Jeffo!"

Top Five Positive and Negative Aspects of Working from Home

Positive

- I feel more relaxed.
- I have a healthier diet.
- I take more time off.
- I exercise more often.
- I have a better mariage and sex life.

Negative

- I have no paid benefits.
- I miss office socializing.
- I have no staff or support.
- I don't get regular raises and bonuses.

Adapted from a 1993 *Home Office Computing* magazine survey.

The ability to get and stay organized is especially important when you don't have the support of a manager or administrative assistant. Working independently requires that you use your time to market your skills or products and deliver them on time. If you are looking for car keys or are moving piles of paper around to find a letter or invoice, you aren't making a living or making a life.

Goal-orientation is high on the list because your clients and customers are the only people monitoring your performance. It's all up to you: what you work on, how much you work, when and how conscientiously you work. You must set achievable goals—such as filling twenty orders a day or writing a report on deadline—while keeping your eye on the bigger strategic goals, such as a gross income figure or a vacation date. You also have to know when enough is enough.

THINGS TO DO TODAY
COMPLETED
DATE
1
2
3
4
5
6
7
8
9
10

Self-confidence and a certain undaunted optimism are vital if, in addition to working at home, you are also in business for yourself, because rejection is a big part of working independently. I maintain this spirit when going after a new project by secretly believing in advance that it is a "done deal." In my mind the first foray—opening the door and presenting my proposal—isn't a sales call, but a first working meeting on the new project. I keep this to myself, but it relaxes me and lets me contribute my expertise freely, without the "please choose me" aura that might otherwise infect my tone. If I don't win the contract, I have still had a good time meeting new people; and, more often than not, they will keep me in mind for another project. Although I'm careful not to give away the expertise I'm paid to deliver, I hold little back and about 80 percent of all the doors I've managed to open have ultimately resulted in contracts, some of which were signed after a year of exchanging phone calls, notes, and small talk.

Decisiveness blossoms from self-confidence and is imperative if you are operating your own business because there may not be anyone higher up to give approval or bail you out if you make a wrong decision. Once I make a willful decision, I surrender to it. This doesn't preclude changing my mind or bailing out if I'm wrong or if the circumstances change, but it does help build momentum and commitment.

An interest in profit is extremely important if you are running your own business because there won't be a salary to depend on. Without a reasonable profit motive, your home-based business may turn into a game you play—pretending to yourself and others that you are making a living. Worse, the IRS will view your activity as a hobby and won't allow you to take deductions for your business expenses if you can't demonstrate that you have been making a serious effort to succeed.

What else is necessary to run a business or career from your home? You must have a high tolerance for handling lots of problems—big and small—seemingly all at the same time. You must be able to cope with uncertainty, as weeks may go by with little or no income; then, suddenly everyone may want what you are selling, and pronto! If you are constantly willing to learn, and if persistence is second nature to you, you are probably well-suited for the home-based business or telecommuter's life. And finally, you should have a bold eye for opportunity and a clear sense of what your personal skills are—along with the ability to connect them to those who can benefit from what you have to offer.

If you don't think you possess enough of these traits, relax, because we will be looking at some tricks of the trade that will help you acquire or strengthen your qualifications. We will also suggest ways to deal with your vulnerabilities. Before long, you will be handling as many successes as problems from the relative sanity of your own personal office.

The Telecommuting Option

Experts generally agree that nearly half the members of the work force in this country are employed in jobs that could be done as well or better somewhere besides an office in a central location. A computer connected to a phone line brings the work to the worker instead of forcing the worker to come to the work. At the same time, telecommuting, as it's often called, gets cars off the road and helps clear the air.

In fact, there is an increasing mandate to implement such flexible options. In December, 1992, San Francisco's Bay Area Air Quality Management District adopted Regulation 13, Rule 1: Trip Reduction Requirements for Large Employers. This requires that all public and private employers with one hundred or more employees at a single work site implement trip reduction programs and promote commuting alternatives, such as ride sharing, public transit, and telecommuting.

The benefits of telecommuting became obvious immediately after the catastrophic 1994 Los Angeles earthquake. Within hours, Pacific Bell, which has had telecommuting programs for its own employees for a number of years, provided a detour around the impassable freeways. They offered free installation and loaner equip-

Working from Home Survey

When asked why they brought work home from the office, respondents said:

- they needed to do extra work or to catch up *(26 percent)*
- it was necessary for the job *(21 percent)*
- they wanted to earn more money *(12 percent)*
- they wanted more time for family *(8 percent)*

When asked how working at home affected their productivity, they said:

- they got much more done at home *(51 percent)*
- their productivity was about the same *(27 percent)*
- they got less done at home *(21 percent)*

When asked about the disadvantages of working at home, they said:

- it was hard to separate personal life and work life *(27 percent)*
- there was less time for themselves *(26 percent)*
- that they worked too much *(24 percent)*
- there was a lack of interaction with co-workers *(24 percent)*
- they lacked the right work equipment *(12 percent)*
- they lacked clerical support *(10 percent)*
- they had less sense of belonging to the company *(7 percent)*

Profile based on a 1992 Link Resources survey.

ment so workers could access the information superhighway and, at the same time, announced major plans to spur telecommuting in the area.

Major Companies Set the Trend

In 1993, *Home Office Computing* magazine reported that there were already 6.6 million telecommuters in the United States, 20 percent more than the year before. A few large companies were experimenting with ways to liberate some of their personnel through telecommuting. One of these companies, Blue Cross/Blue Shield of South Carolina, instituted a program that gave employees personal computers to take home to process the company's medical-claims data and paid them by the number of claims processed. The employees worked as many hours as they wished, whenever they wished, and were paid according to the number of claims they processed.

Control Data Corporation launched the Homework Program, installing computer terminals in the homes of employees with disabilities who were trained in computer programming. The employees write software at home and send it in over telephone lines. Continental Illinois Bank has a similar program for employees who transcribe recorded dictation that is sent to them by telephone. The processed text is then sent in to the bank's mainframe computer, again via phone lines, and printed out at headquarters.

These early pilot programs proved that morale and productivity could be increased measurably when employees work at home. Today, management personnel whose responsibilities do not require five days a week of face-to-face communication are exercising similar options. In 1993, Arthur Andersen and Company, the international accounting and consulting firm, supplied a third of its accountants with powerful laptop computers and sent them home. The computers, equipped with spreadsheet and presentation graphics software, plus capabilities for plugging into networks of other computers and databases, gave the accountants much more client contact. Piloted in Los Angeles, it worked so well that the program is now operational in Dallas, Houston, Chicago, and Minneapolis, and will soon be company-wide. Many corporations that encourage telecommuting not only provide their employees with computers and modems but home office furniture and equipment as well.

You don't have to be a telecommuter to work at home. Your job may not be adaptable to telecommuting; your temperament may not be suited to working alone five days a week. In the latter case, you might want to consider flexible scheduling, an increasingly popular option that can include job-sharing, a compressed work week, or working from home only part-time.

In 1993, New York's Aetna Life and Casualty began considering the changing demographics of its work force. They discovered that by the year 2000, about two-thirds of their employees will be women, and 75 percent of those women will become pregnant at least once during their working years. As an experiment, Aetna created a special, full-time arrangement for a personnel manager who was about to have a baby. She now works three ten-hour days and puts in the remaining ten hours of her forty-hour week at home. If the program is successful, Aetna will be prepared to accommodate the changes ahead. Unfortunately, the benefits of telecommuting and flexible work schedules have not yet been universally accepted.

Work Family Directions, a Boston-based consulting group, surveyed eighty companies in late 1993 and found that 85 percent of them offered at least one flexible work program. However, among those companies, only 2 percent of the employees actually used the programs. According to Fran Rodgers, chief executive officer of the group, managers resist flexible options for fear that productivity will drop—even though most studies show the opposite—and because alternative schedules are harder to keep track of. Rodgers reports that flexible scheduling "is still seen as a favor to a valued employee, even though the evidence shows people are more productive when they are given flexibility."

Making It Work for You

You might have to do some homework to convince your company to let you start working from home. But take heart. Many of the programs already in place were instigated by workers. If you want to pitch telecommuting to your employer, analyze your job and write up a telecommuting job description citing the many successful precedents. Set up a way to account for your time by establishing milestones, deadlines, and deliverables, so your manager won't think you are really watching the ball game when you should be working. Propose a way to ease into the situation. You might want to start with one half-day a week at home which, after two months, would grow to two full days a week, which is how often the average American telecommuter works from home. A number of city governments are now offering tax incentives to companies who support telecommuting, just as they have for car pooling. If yours is one, the tax advantage for your company may be the clincher for your proposal. You can even videotape your home office to show your employer that you do have a place to get the work done. And you might also get together with your work group to organize a team of potential telecommuters to present to management. Go for it. The worst thing your employer can do is say no.

There is a downside to telecommuting, particularly for anyone wrapped up in dreams of advancement. According to Gil Gordon, a telecommuting consultant, "If their ultimate goal is to move up as long and as far as possible, they will spend more time at home obsessing about not rubbing elbows with the VP in the lunch line, their work will suffer, and their worries will be self-fulfilling."

You can maintain visibility by making sure your work at home produces a significant benefit to your boss and the company. Keep an eye open for opportunities to advance your employer's interests to demonstrate that you aren't just cocooning somewhere. Stay in touch with your management, and remind them from time to time how well the arrangement is working for you—and prove it with superior work. Remain flexible about how you do your work for the firm, just as they are being flexible by allowing you to work at home part-time. By looking out for your company from afar, you will shine brightly even from the distance of your home.

You may miss the proverbial water-cooler gossip. More seriously, you may find that when it comes to company politics, the player who is out of sight may be dangerously out of the minds of staff and management. This is why you should arrange to be on site a little more than required—not just to maintain your territory in the company culture, but to enjoy the stimulation of colleagues and to keep up the brainstorming that can enrich your work. When you are in your home office, use the phone to keep in touch. Don't let your role in the company become merely "virtual."

For millions, the positive aspects of working from home part-time far outweigh the disadvantages. Being able to take a break for an hour in the morning to work in the garden or to swim twenty laps contributes to a happier, less stressful, more productive professional life. This in turn enriches your family life, the best protection against burnout over the long run. At the very least, telecommuting can help you find out whether you are temperamentally suited to working from home exclusively or to working for yourself. It may be the perfect transitional step to complete independence down the road.

Resources

For further support, contact Work Family Directions, 930 Commonwealth Avenue W, Boston, MA 02215-1274. (617) 278-4000.

Telecommuting: A Handbook to Help You Set Up a Program at Your Company, prepared by the California Department of Transportation in cooperation with the U.S. Department of Transportation, Federal Highway Administration, is a good tool for proposing a telecommuting program to your company. The handbook provides a procedure by which a telecommuting program can be designed and implemented, and it includes successful case studies. Available from RIDES for Bay Area Commuters, Inc. (415) 861-7665.

Telecommuting Guidelines for Telecommuters and Telecommuting Guidelines for Supervisors are concise workbooks to help you and your supervisor create a telecommuting program. Available from Economic Development Partnership, Inc., 2150 Webster Street, Room 1000, Oakland, CA 94612. (510) 645-0673.

The Telecommuter's Handbook: How to Work for a Salary—Without Ever Leaving the House. Brad Schepp describes the jobs best suited for telecommuting, names and addresses of more than 100 companies that allow employees to work at home, and the pros and cons of telecommuting for both employee and employer. Pharos books: A Scripps Howard Company, 200 Park Avenue, New York, NY 10166.

Telecommuting Review, edited and published by Gil Gordon, offers in-depth looks at national and international telecommuting issues, including trip-reduction legislation, union rules, and the results of telecommuting programs in local and national companies. This 14-page monthly newsletter is available for $157 annually, from Telespan Publishing Corporation, 50 West Palm Street, Altadena, CA 91001. (818) 797-5482.

Starting a Home-Based Business

If you are the home office type, you are probably the entrepreneurial type as well and may be ready to head out on your own.

One advantage of keeping a salaried job while pursuing independent business goals is that your company salary can give you the financial stability and continuity required for you to ease into your own home-based business.

Based on his own experience, Robert Ortalda now counsels would-be home workers to establish an income-producing home office while still working at a full-time job to avoid the shock of being out of a job one day and having to earn a living from scratch the next. By making the transition from a weekday routine gradual, you, your family, and friends will adjust with less stress and more enjoyment. I recommend setting up at least a minimal home office—even if it doesn't yet harbor a business—to provide a life raft to jump into in case of emergency, rather than having to sit in your car or a bar with a pink slip in your hand.

Top Ten Reasons for Starting Your Own Business

1. I wanted to be my own boss.
2. I wanted less routine in my life.
3. I wanted more interesting work.
4. I wanted to change my life.
5. I disliked the corporate world.
6. I wanted more family time.
7. I wanted to make more money.
8. I had a great idea.
9. I'd gone as far as I could at my job.
10. I lost my job.

From a 1993 survey conducted by *Home Office Computing* magazine.

If you think it's rough worrying about losing your salaried position, consider how much more stressful it can be to depend on the erratic nature of your own business when it's your face that's out there and your friends and family who are monitoring your dream. With most regular jobs, you may at least qualify for a few months of unemployment benefits, but with your own business, you may not even qualify for food stamps if you need them!

If you have a spouse, one of you would ideally remain salaried to maintain some financial security. If you will be taking the plunge together, first save as many months of operating money as possible before getting out on the self-employment limb to avoid the duress of irregular, nonsalary income. Then, to make sure your success isn't gained at the expense of your relationship, sit down with your spouse and have a patient, realistic discussion. "What if one of us is laid off? What if the business isn't bringing in a profit and the mortgage is past due and a dental bill is looming?" Try to reach a mutual understanding, and take notes that will form the basis of an agreement, a social contract between you and your spouse—and your children, if you have any.

Focus on Your Destination

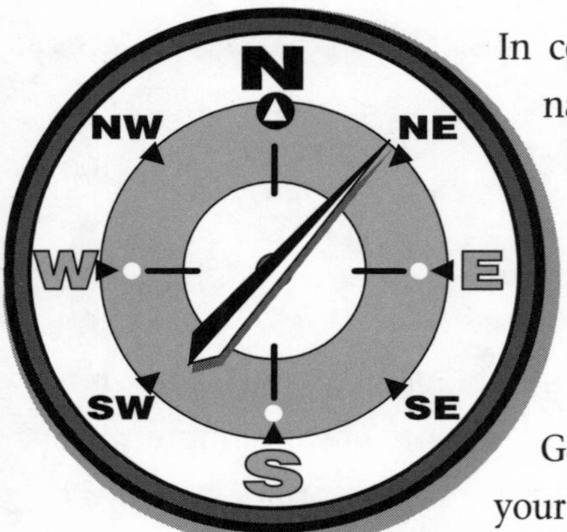

In colonial Salem, Massachusetts, an ordinance made it illegal for anyone to set out without knowing where they were going. Although it seems absurd today, it's not a bad law to observe when you are starting a new venture.

Get your bearings, and start focusing on your destination. But before you head out, ask yourself two questions: What are the unique qualities or services I can bring to the marketplace? Is there a real need for this type of business?

The choice of what independent business or profession to launch is best based on what you already know how to do and, hopefully, what you really enjoy doing. If you have a green thumb, you have probably dreamt of being a landscape designer. If you are a systems analyst for a company, you may be tempted to launch yourself as a consultant in the same field. If you love having house guests, a bed-and-breakfast business might sound like heaven to you. Perhaps you are a great cook. You could start a catering service or bake pastries for local coffee shops.

Just having a talent or passion for something doesn't ensure there's a market for it. This may require a little basic research. Worry not; it's easier than it sounds.

The Top Ten Home-Based Businesses

1. Business consulting and services
2. Computer services and programming
3. Financial consulting and services
4. Marketing and advertising
5. Medical practice and services
6. Graphics and visual arts
7. Public relations and publicity
8. Real estate
9. Writing
10. Independent sales

Source: Link Resources, Inc.

Robert Bloom, who lives about forty miles west of Chicago, was in data processing and systems development for twenty-five years before deciding to look into electronic medical-claims processing. In this business, independent contractors handle Medicare, Blue Cross, and other medical claims for doctors who are already buried in paperwork. A number of companies sell turn-key systems that include everything needed to run this type of business. But before changing careers and investing in the software and licensing fees required to launch the service, Bloom did some serious market research in his community.

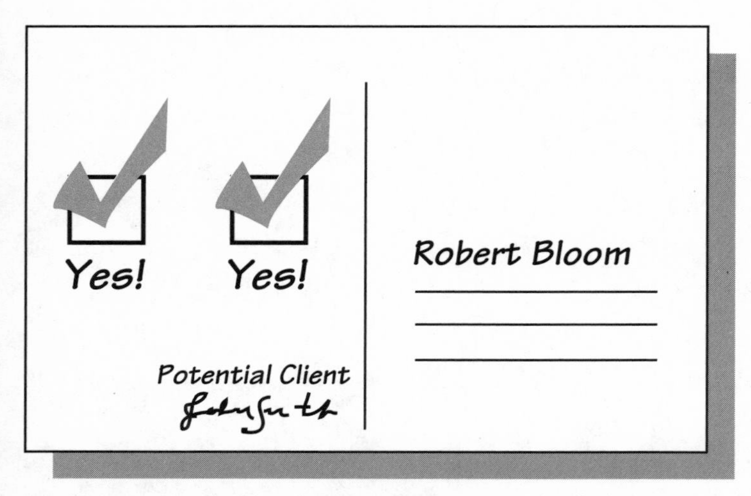

He sent out a hundred questionnaires, with five yes-or-no questions, on a self-addressed, stamped postcard to a random list of doctors and dentists. Within a few days, he received thirty-three responses from offices interested in learning more about his electronic claims-processing service. He continued to send slightly different questionnaires every few weeks to those medical offices that hadn't responded—always emphasizing the benefits of his services—until he was confident that there was a market for the business he wanted to launch. For the price of a few stamps, Bloom got the feedback he needed. He began by signing up two doctors and has built his business slowly, carefully, and successfully ever since.

However, even having the vital elements of talent, passion, and a waiting market won't ensure that your business will be successful. You'll find out more about creating your own business in Chapter 9. Meanwhile, let's explore how you can set up an office and organize your time to maximize your chances of successfully balancing your business or profession with the rest of your life.

Resources

Paul and Sarah Edwards have written a valuable resource guide, *The Best Home Businesses for the '90s* (Jeremy P. Tarcher, 1991), that details how the most viable home businesses work, their approximate earning potential, and the knowledge and skills you should have for each.

If you are one of the many thousands of executives and middle managers suddenly out of work, you may decide to market your skills by starting your own consulting service. If so, *Selling Your Services: Proven Strategies for Getting Clients to Hire You or Your Firm* by Robert W. Bly (Henry Holt and Co.) is a valuable resource. Bly, a veteran copywriter and author, provides upbeat, practical tips for anyone trying to sell their services.

If you are still looking for inspiration, you'll enjoy reading Paul Hawken's classic *Growing a Business* (Simon and Schuster, 1986) written for those running or wishing to run their own business completely outside the corporate world. The author co-founded the phenomenally successful mail-order garden supply house Smith & Hawken. His most recent book, *The Ecology of Commerce: A Declaration of Sustainability,* is a practical guide for using commerce as an agent for change. One of Hawken's main themes is that business is the one mechanism powerful enough to reverse global environmental and social degradation.

"The Small Business Development Catalog," published by *Entrepreneur* Magazine, offers more than 150 business guides to everything from mobile bookkeeping services to wedding planning. If you are unsure about where to start, just skimming the titles of possible businesses listed in the index may inspire you. Most of the guides cost about sixty dollars. Some have available related videos and software, and all come with a thirty-day refund guarantee. Entrepreneur Group, 2392 Morse Avenue, P.O. Box 19787, Irvine, CA 92713-9787. (800) 421-2300.

Organizing Your Space for Fun and Profit

Many people who set up a home office are so anxious to get started that they plunk down their equipment, notebooks, and card files on the biggest surface they can find—often the dining room table. Whatever you do, don't start working there. Almost everyone who does discovers that they never get their table back for dining! On the other hand, you may eventually find yourself using the dining table or spreading out in the living room once in a while for a change of scene.

Keep in mind that, in opening up a new physical space in which to work, you are also creating a psychological space where you will be living and doing what you do best.

An Early Home Office

Thomas Jefferson, America's third president (1801–1809), was way ahead of his time when he created his estate at Monticello. This great American Renaissance man designed an integrated office-bedroom and anticipated many features that have since become standard requirements in today's home offices, including a swivel chair and foot rest, task lighting in the form of candles on the arms of the chair, a "data base" on a revolving bookstand that allowed him to have four books open at once, and a pantograph, the personal copying machine of the eighteenth century.

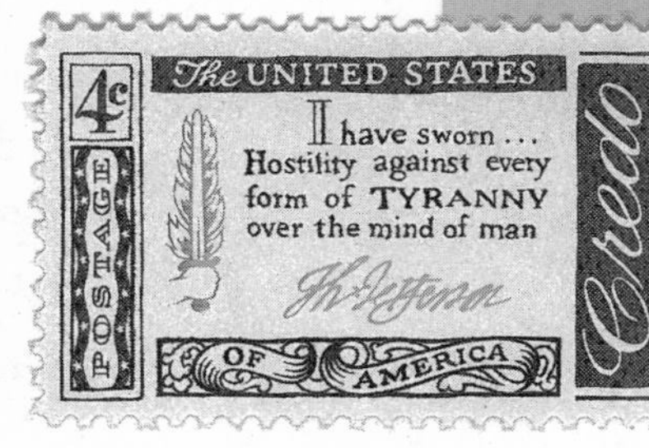

You will need to create a separate environment where you go to work, a zone where you won't be interrupted by friends or family—especially if there are children in the household. The minimum space you'll need for a desk, chair, and file cabinet is six feet by eight feet.

The most important item of home office equipment—whether you live in an apartment or a palace—is a door that closes! If you live in a studio apartment, you can partition off a corner of the main room with a Japanese-style *shoji* screen so when your work is done, you can at least visually close your office. If you don't physically enclose your space, your work will be staring at you around the clock—while you eat, watch television, visit with family and friends, and try to sleep.

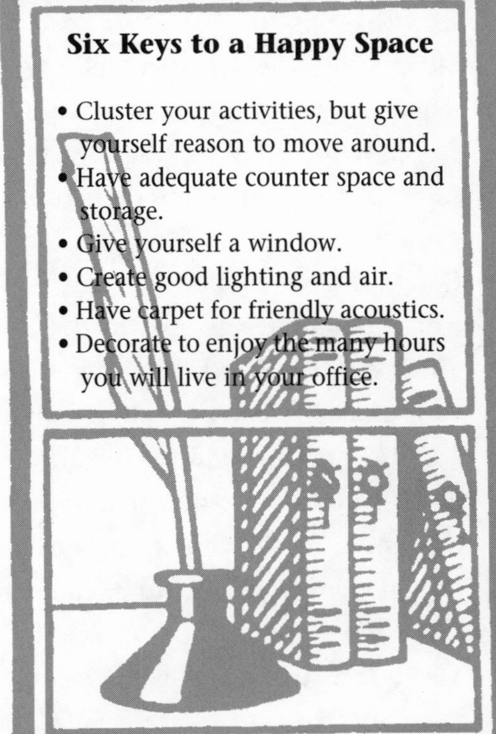

Six Keys to a Happy Space

- Cluster your activities, but give yourself reason to move around.
- Have adequate counter space and storage.
- Give yourself a window.
- Create good lighting and air.
- Have carpet for friendly acoustics.
- Decorate to enjoy the many hours you will live in your office.

Another option is to purchase office furniture that is designed to close up to hide everything. One furniture maker, Basset, builds an armoire with a fold-down desk and interior space for a computer, monitor, printer, and keyboard tray. Techline, dak, and Dimensions, among others, offer modular, multifunction furniture that allows you to change the configuration at will.

If possible, use a separate room for your office that will be relatively safe from interruptions. Liberate a spare bedroom, den, or garage space. The more removed it is from the activity center where family and friends are, the better. If you choose a garage, make sure it is comfortable, particularly in extremes of weather. But don't be tempted to take over the basement or attic; you don't want to spend your new life in a dungeon. Remember that you are liberating yourself, not digging in.

If you have the space and budget, you can remodel your home or build an addition designed by an architect with some experience in home offices. It can be an exciting creative challenge, but elaborate measures aren't necessary for creating a successful personal office.

My own office is rather compact. I deliberately set it up so that I am required to get out of my chair to get to the fax machine and laser printer. I have to stretch to reach my scissors and must stand to grab other supplies. This setup keeps me active while I'm working with my mind.

Good space use has much more to do with how you arrange things than with the absolute size of your space. If an astronaut can perform well in a tiny but fiercely efficient area, surely you will be able to manage in your available space! If you design your office so your most frequent activities are all within reach, either in a corner (preferably with a window) or around an L- or U-shaped desk, you can use a smaller space more efficiently. Consider how a kitchen is set up for efficient use of space: the close proximity of sink, stove, and refrigerator saves time and energy.

Make It Your Space

Once you have chosen your sanctuary zone, try not to imitate the cold, efficient look of workaday offices. Create a comfortable atmosphere, which might include posters and other art that is often forbidden in corporate office settings.

An aquarium is a relaxing addition, and potted plants, miniature trees, and other greenery will keep you in touch with nature and help clear the air of environmental pollutants. Taking care of a few plants and fish will also provide pleasant and productive breaks for you during your work day or work night. If you don't have a green thumb, keep cut flowers on your desk. A clump of wildflowers will bring as much eye joy to your office as a florist's bouquet.

Plants require good lighting, and so do you. Try to mix daylight with full-spectrum ambient lights for the overall space, and use small task lights for reading and by the phone. Avoid fluorescent lights, high-frequency strobes that often cause eyestrain and headaches.

Fresh air is as important as good light. While modern offices are built with sealed windows and recirculate the air inside, you can set up your personal office with fresh air from the outside if you live in a relatively unpolluted community. You may want to install an air conditioner or ceiling fan. Don't skimp when it comes to your comfort and health.

Try to situate your desk with a window on one side or the other, rather than in back or in front of you. If you are using a computer, this positioning is essential to avoid screen reflection and glare. Even without a computer, situating yourself near a window offers visual relief while you are sitting at your desk. If you have no view, hang landscape paintings or photographic posters that let your mind out of the room occasionally.

Add enough shades, drapes, or curtains to maintain your privacy and security. Carpets or rugs will make walking and standing more comfortable and will baffle the sound of computers, fax machines, phones, and footsteps. Avoid carpets containing synthetics and petrochemicals, which generate static electricity as you walk and give off chemical exhausts that can trigger allergies for years.

Decorate to please your personal taste, making your space as inviting for you as for visitors. By creating a delightful place to spend your eight or more hours a day, self-discipline will be much easier and you'll find yourself looking forward to that ten-second commute.

Once you have the space, organize your personal office in a way that strikes the balance between military orderliness and absolute chaos that suits your personal working style. Good chefs cluster their tools, and they clean as they go. By the time they sit down to enjoy the results of their efforts, the kitchen is tidy. Albert Einstein, on the other hand, inhabited an especially messy office at Princeton University. When a journalist visited him and asked how the father of modern atomic physics could work in such chaos, he replied, "It's meaningful chaos." Fortunately, Einstein had genius on his side—and he didn't have to entertain potential clients in his office.

There is hardly an office on earth, from an architect's office to a novelist's cottage, that has enough flat work surface. Like closet space, you never have enough; when you add more, it fills up almost before the paint dries. If you can, set up more desktop and counter area than you think you'll ever need. I guarantee you'll use it.

Contrary to the ads, there is no such thing as a paperless office, so you'll need at least one four-drawer file cabinet. The best cabinets have full suspension arms that support the length of each drawer and hang each file on side rails; with other types, you'll wind up with files that slouch in the drawer and are difficult to separate and find. Filed items can easily fall victim to the file-and-forget syndrome, so riffle through them regularly.

If your documents are sensitive, such as medical claims to be processed for payment, be sure your file drawers can be locked to avoid the liability that could ensue if the records fell into the wrong hands. A fireproof file cabinet might provide extra peace of mind for other more sensitive documents. You might also consider purchasing a fire-proof safe that can't be lugged away and will withstand an hour-long fire. A good place to install one is behind a false wall or bookcase, or embedded in cement in an out-of-the-way part of your garage floor. You may want to rent a safe-deposit box in your local bank for safe-guarding sensitive business data when you travel out of town. It's also a good place to store computer disks, because the heat from an hour-long house fire would melt them even in a fire-proof safe. I always leave home with a small floppy disk of my most important materials in my jacket pocket. They are extremely valuable because of all the time and toil that went into their creation.

Wall-mounted plastic or wooden folder holders are great for keeping current projects, invoices, letters, and news clippings within view and reach without taking up valuable desk or counter space. You only have to look up from your work to be reminded of your most active projects.

Neat freaks and lovers of relative chaos agree that a terrific way to prevent important things from disappearing under piles of other stuff is to buy inexpensive plastic briefcases in a variety of colors and put everything pertaining to a single project in its own case. You can go right to the blue briefcase to file incoming materials and to the gray case to grab the project for those manufacturers in Minneapolis. These cases usually cost less than lunch and can save you many hours.

Small bookcases are useful for storing envelopes and stationery, printer paper, tape, glue, and other items you want within reach. This way they are out of the way but still in view. Your incoming mail, new magazines, and current newspapers should be left out in the open to keep them from sinking to the bottom of your personal tar pit.

Depending on what type of business you have, you may want some general storage space for oversize shipping envelopes, blueprints, product samples, copier toner, phone books, and other stuff that should be kept close at hand but out of the way. A closet is often the best solution. It's essential to avoid wading through a clutter every time you want to refer to an item, make a knowledgeable phone call, or fax a document.

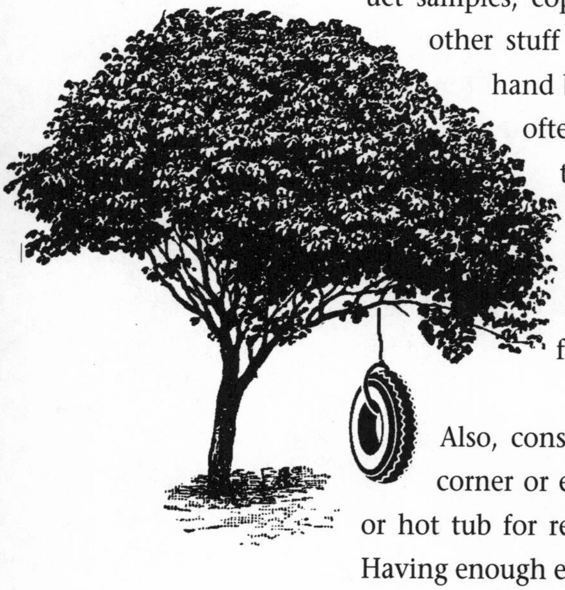

Also, consider the value of an exercise corner or even an entire room, or a spa or hot tub for relief from marathon sessions. Having enough entertainment in your home—

especially a good sound system—can help you resist going out on overly long breaks.

You'll want to purchase and store adequate supplies, too. Managing your supply of little items can be as vital to getting the big things out the door as managing your time is. Feeding your fax, printer, copier, and other business-support equipment is what keeps *you* fed. If you run out of fax paper just as a contract is coming in from Colorado Springs, the delay will make you look unprofessional and could cost you important business. So stock up on manila and shipping envelopes, presentation binders, filing and organizing supplies, report covers, tape, staples, and fax paper. Try to stay one unit ahead on toner cartridges for your laser printer and copier machine and about six units ahead on ribbons for your dot-matrix printer and typewriter. You don't have to buy enough supplies to last until your grandchildren are too old to play shuffleboard, but you should buy them in quantities large enough to minimize surprises. It's especially important if you live a half-hour drive from the nearest supplier, as I do. Having five thousand more staples than you think you'll ever use is far better than having just one too few!

Evaluate Your Space

Once you are up and running for a few weeks, reassess how well you are using your space.

- Do you still have enough surface area for folders, papers, invoices, letters, and current projects?
- Are your wall-mounted folder holders being used well, or are you just stashing magazines in them?
- Are you letting things pile up? (Of course you are. Everyone does. But are you constantly hunting for items and papers you need?)
- Can you get to the fax machine easily, or do you have to close the lower file cabinet drawer before you can reach that incoming message without bruising your shin?

Even if you are doing quite well, give yourself a space-use upgrade every now and then by taking a morning or a day to analyze and reorganize your productivity center. In an extreme case, move everything out, and then move back in again for a fresh start.

Resources

These books can guide you in creating a healthful home office environment. After all, you don't want to exchange the toxic corporate world for something equally unhealthful inside your home.

Take Time to Organize

The National Association of Professional Organizers has declared every January tenth as National Clean Off Your Desk Day. According to the association, people with messy desk habits can expect to take three months to establish a new behavior pattern.

Healing Environments: Your Guide to Indoor Well-Being, by Carol Venolia (Celestial Arts, 1988), includes chapters on light, color, sound and noise, indoor air quality, the thermal environment, plants and gardens, and other subjects.

Office Work Can Be Dangerous to Your Health, by Jeanne Stellman, Ph.D., and Mary Sue Henifin, M.P.H. (Pantheon Books, 1983), covers the effects of lighting, video display terminals, photocopiers, and other common office machines, plus a wide range of other things to consider for maximum health while working.

The Non-Toxic Home, by Debra Lynn Dadd (Tarcher/St. Martin's Press, 1986), covers tap water, pesticides, plastics, furnishings and appliances, and toxic house plants.

Ion and Light Company is a complete supplier of environmentally friendly air and water purifying products, plus full-spectrum light bulbs. Ion and Light Company, 2263-1/2 Sacramento Street, San Francisco, CA 94115. (415) 346-6205.

If your car is your office, Modular Trunk Products sells CAR-GO-FILE, an automobile trunk organizing system for books, catalogs, samples, or tools. For a brochure, write MTP, P.O. Box 973, Newark, CA 94560, or call (800) 426-3453.

Motivation and Self-Discipline

Working in the privacy of your home office can put you in dangerous proximity to the refrigerator, the television, and the bed. Many home businesses have suffered serious setbacks from a six-pack of beer and televised baseball. Almost every human being has a budding bad habit of some kind, and if you are spending too much time alone with an eating disorder or are dependent on tobacco or some other substance, working alone can make the habit blossom. While your workday should be spiced up with occasional breaks, indulging bad habits can sink you before you start. Don't let little weaknesses steal the freedom you have gained. If there ever was a time to emphasize self-discipline, it is the first day you go to work at home.

Some years ago a magazine cartoon showed a writer at his typewriter with a winged muse perched on his right shoulder saying, "Well done! Keep it up!" At the same time, a little devil was on his left shoulder saying, "Hey! Whadayou say we go get a beer and a sandwich!" We all have little "friends" sitting on our shoulders admonishing us about this and that. Which you listen to will determine how successful you will be at maintaining the discipline required to keep a healthy balance between enterprise and leisure.

You may find that one of the biggest joys of working from home is the freedom to work all day in a bathrobe—until the day an important prospect or account drops in unexpectedly. Your embarrassment will be compounded if your home is a mess as well. A home-based accountant I know deliberately gets ready for work each morning by "dressing for success." When suited for action, he sees himself as ready for anything. He also keeps his home looking like a showplace by day, though it may become more comfortably rumpled toward evening. I want my own home to look good for myself most of the time because I spend a large part of my life there. I have a mirror by my desk so when I look up from my writing I can see that I'm "on deck," present and accounted for. This visual, positive feedback reminds me daily that a big part of success is showing up. "You must be present to win" is especially true when you are in business for yourself.

"You must be present to win"

Staying on Track

Procrastination and simple laziness come all too easy in the privacy of a home office. If you find yourself procrastinating, do the most unpleasant thing at the beginning of the day so you don't spend the rest of the day building resistance. Do one thing at a time rather than thinking about all the things you have to do.

Every day, create a to-do list to manage your activities. Prioritize it, putting the most important things first and the stuff you can do any time at the end. If you make your list the night before, you will be far less prone to spending restless hours in the dark worrying about all the things you have to do tomorrow or rehearsing how you will do them. If you can't sleep, get up and take care of one of tomorrow's tasks. Then you can return to bed with a sense of accomplishment and use the time you saved to sleep in.

However, don't let making the list substitute for doing what's on the list. And don't make long, endlessly detailed lists that will overwhelm you and make you give up before you start. Set achievable goals for the day and you will accomplish more with less stress. The simple act of checking off each item as you complete it will give you a great deal of satisfaction. What you don't accomplish will simply get moved to the next day's list. If you are interrupted or simply call it quits for the day, write yourself a next-action note so you know where you left off and you can pick up the beat when you return to work. Whatever happens, don't be too hard on yourself. As someone once put it, "Forget about perfection. Excellence will do!"

Set achievable goals for the day and you will accomplish more with less stress.

Maintaining your own style of structure and continuity is a source of power and success. For example, you may always find it easier to pick up where you left off than to start fresh each day; if so, deliberately leave a job unfinished so you won't begin the next day staring at a blank page.

Some high achievers practice a kind of yoga to stay motivated. It centers on imagining the positive results they will reap at the end of their project—instead of getting too focused on individual tasks. Suppose you have to create a business plan to obtain an investment from a partner or bank. The task may not be fun, but imagine the pleasure of having a decent bank account to draw on when you need to buy equipment, print a brochure, or travel to Europe. Picture yourself sitting at a Paris bistro on Boulevard Saint-Michel, closing an important deal with a new client. Imagine that you are banking profits, taking vacations, and donating to charity. This imaging can power you through the gray zones. Marathon runners use positive imagery to picture themselves breaking the ribbon at the finish line. If it can work for them for twenty grueling miles, it can certainly help you through a few tedious tasks.

On the flip side, you can motivate yourself by imagining the negative consequences of not accomplishing the task before you. If you don't get the funding, you may wind up with no business or professional life, or living in the basement of your maiden aunt's ranch, snowbound in the winter with a broken TV, no mail delivery, and no phone of your own. Or worse.

If you find yourself faltering or suffering a creative block, get active on something completely unrelated. Take a short walk or swim. The exercise will do you good, the fresh air will clear your mind, and getting out of the house will put distance between you and the refrigerator. If you find the fridge has a magnetic pull, take a tip from the weight-loss gurus: The moment you find yourself heading for the magic door, glance at your watch and decide to stay away for at least ten minutes. When you return, you may find that the urge has gone.

Whatever you do to keep the ball rolling, once you accomplish a major goal or groups of little goals, reward yourself. Celebrate! Watch the game, have a picnic in the park, take a walk, go swimming, or go out to lunch. Mix with your community.

Most people are surprised to learn that one of the biggest challenges to the freedom won by working at home is the compulsion to work endlessly. In *The Overworked American,* economist Juliet B. Schor reports that we give ourselves less vacation time than any country in the industrialized world. Italians get four to six weeks a year; the Finns, French, and Germans get five to six. By contrast, Americans get approximately four weeks. Our national habit is to work. You'll be happier and more productive in the long run if you take some time off. Plan ahead for a vacation by training someone to take over for a while. Remember: you are working to live.

7 Managing Your Time Effectively

"For tribal man space was the uncontrollable mystery," Marshall McLuhan once said. "For technological man it is time that occupies the same role."

In a 1990 Gallup poll, more people complained about a feeling of "time poverty" than a shortage of money. Precious moments at home are constantly interrupted by phone calls, junk mail, and knocks at the door, and radio and TV advertising shouting that "Time's running out! Only three days left!" It's worse if you are trying to work. But even without these obnoxious interruptions, controlling how you use your time can be surprisingly difficult. Neighbors, family, and friends might see that you are "home" all the time and think it's okay to pop in to ask you to help them move their refrigerator in the middle of your workday.

Kim Delon, a home-based magazine subscription fulfillment worker reports that a major benefit of working at home is that her children can see how she earns a living and value and respect Mom's work. But first she had to tame her family's impulse to barge into her office at any time. "We had a joke that they could only interrupt me in case of an emergency," she says, "something involving blood or smoke—and a lot of it."

e of the first things you must do to establish a successful home office is to help your family and friends understand that even though you are working at home, you are really "at the office" during certain hours, and ask them to respect that. By securing their cooperation ahead of time, you won't offend them by resisting their intrusions into your sanctuary. Family and friends must respect your working hours—even if those hours aren't regular. Make an OFFICE HOURS sign for your office door or the space you have set aside, and hang it up every time you go to work. Display times on the sign if you keep regular hours. If you don't have a door, hang the sign on the wall by your desk. A variation is a two-sided sign that displays BUSY and FREE.

Many "open collar" workers find that because they are so close to their desks, the workday often never ends. They may become so absorbed in their projects that they don't break loose and "commute" back home to the living room, or their colleagues may call for business reasons in the dead of night or on weekends.

Give as much respect to your private time as you do your business hours. Even just hearing an answering machine pick up a call while you are eating dinner, playing with your children, or sitting in front of the fireplace with your spouse can break the magic. So, put only your business phone number on your business cards, and turn off your answering machine's speaker after hours. Better yet, subscribe to a computerized message service if your local phone company provides it.

Maintaining your private time zone can become more complicated if you are doing business across time zones and date lines, but you can confine these time-warp communications to faxes that can be sent on a delayed, automatic basis while you sleep.

If you are trading stocks and bonds, or commodity trading by computer and modem in "real time," setting aside normal hours for home life can be more difficult—especially if your spouse works a regular job. In this case, a separate room well out of hearing range is essential.

You can take advantage of different time zones to save money. For example, I try to make phone calls from my Pacific Coast home to East Coast and European clients before 8 A.M. Pacific time, and to Hawaii and Asia after 5 P.M. (but well before my dinner). They are already at work, and phones rates are significantly lower.

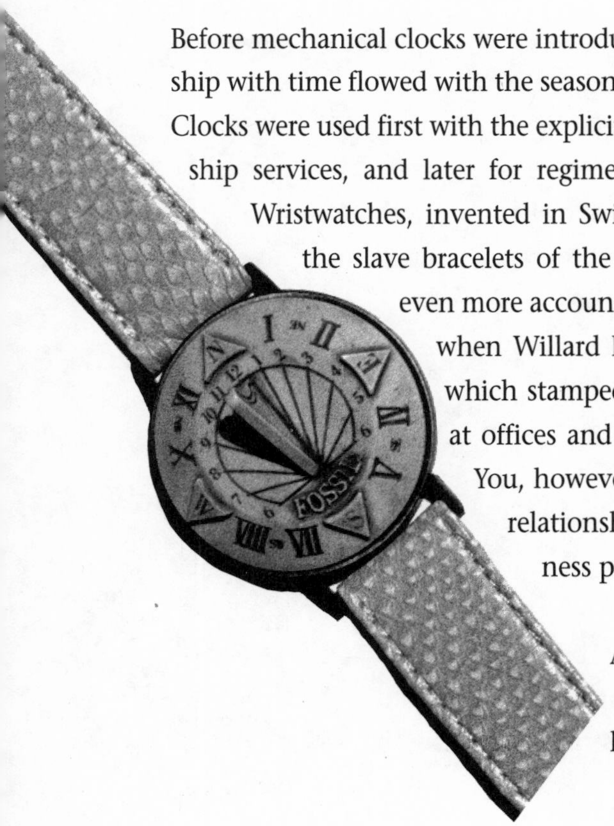

Before mechanical clocks were introduced in the late 1650s, our relationship with time flowed with the seasons, the sun, the moon, and the stars. Clocks were used first with the explicit purpose of regulating church worship services, and later for regimenting factory workers and clerks. Wristwatches, invented in Switzerland in 1790, quickly became the slave bracelets of the industrial revolution. We became even more accountable to clocks and watches in 1888 when Willard L. Bundy invented the time clock, which stamped workers' cards as they clocked in at offices and factories, and is still in use today. You, however, will enjoy a much more flexible relationship with time as a home-based business person.

Adopting a somewhat philosophical attitude towards time can help you balance yourself between the temptations of sloth and workaholism. Don't let time drive your work. Instead, let your newfound wealth of time nurture your activity, and you'll find that your workday will become so inspired it's like sailing "in the slot" or jogging "in the zone." One hour of enthusiastic activity can accomplish far more than eight hours of drudgery.

Our word *enthusiasm* comes from the Greek words meaning "the God within"—which can mean "the god of creativity," the "enterprising god," or whatever muse gives you those Aha! insights that move you to focused action. Be careful that you don't turn into a driven, compulsive workaholic who can't sit still for a moment or give your family the same kind of attention you lavish on agendas and computer screens. Why trade a life of beehive productivity in an office building for a hamster cage in your home? Hop off the spinning clock face, and taste the power of "natural" time.

Do remember, however, that respecting the time and schedules of clients, customers, and suppliers is required for success, even as your own time-sense mellows. Not everyone else will have the same freedom as you, especially 9-to-5ers. This can be especially tough on those who are dividing their time between a company and a home office, or if one spouse works at home and the other in a corporate office.

At the very least, respect the time demands of the salaried world if your business depends on deadlines. You may not have to watch the clock, but you must observe the calendar. Expect every project to take longer than anticipated, and if you have deadlines, plan backward. Start with the date delivery is due and work backward, allowing extra time at each step for unexpected delays and rest periods. Once you've figured out when you must start, do so!

If you are dividing your time between a company job outside and your own business, you must dedicate yourself to your own business or professional interests only on your own time. A perfect prescription for disaster is to make business phone calls for your personal enterprise at your employer's expense, and taking such calls at work will cause a royal mess.

If you divide your time between a corporate and a home office, avoid the temptation to plunge into your personal office as soon as you get home. Make time to tickle your two-year-old or to sit down to a real meal with your partner before you retire to your working sanctuary.

When tempted to run from store to store to save money on purchases, take a lesson from professionals and tradespeople who charge hourly rates: It doesn't pay to make a one-hour round trip to shop where office supplies are cheaper if your hour is worth the fifty dollars you save. Instead, shop closer to home even if you have to pay a higher price, and use the time you save to do something profitable and enjoyable. If you must spend a lot of time behind the wheel for any reason, occasionally listen to a tape about subjects that will enhance your personal or business knowledge.

Back at your office, filter out the things you don't need, and organize the rest. Try not to fiddle around with junk mail looking for that ever-elusive ten million dollars that *somebody's* going to win. If you are self-employed, you are already a winner by virtue of not having to ask anyone when your next vacation is scheduled or if you may please take Monday off!

Time Is Life

If you think you waste a lot of time standing in line and sitting in traffic, you are probably right, according to Michael Fortino, president of the consulting firm Priority Management Pittsburgh. Most people spend five years of their life waiting in lines and six months sitting at traffic lights! Fortino's researchers studied hundreds of people across the nation for more than a year and found that the average person spends eight months opening junk mail, one year searching for misplaced objects, two years trying to return telephone calls to people who never seem to be in, and four years doing housework.

"Most people don't realize how much time they're wasting," Fortino says. "The whole point is to spend time doing the things that you want to do rather than the things you dislike."

Fortino suggests the following ways to save time and reduce stress:

- Spend eight to ten minutes at the end of each workday making realistic lists of the most important things to be done the next day.
- Make use of time spent waiting by carrying reading material or other projects with you.
- Plan travel routes and times, and listen to traffic reports to avoid delays.
- Have a place for everything at home and at work, especially often-used items such as glasses and keys.

Fortino's advice can help you avoid wasting time. But you will be wasting the joy of self-employment or telecommuting if you live and work with a "parking meter" attitude about time.

Don't Fall Into the "Futz Factor"

Two percent of America's gross domestic product—ninety-seven billion dollars—is "futzed away" by workers tinkering with their computers, messing around with typefaces, trying to link computers, developing overly elaborate spreadsheets, and endlessly polishing charts, graphs, and other things that would make a great impression—if they ever got done.

From a recent study by SBT, a Sausalito, California accounting software manufacturer.

Benjamin Franklin wasn't completely accurate when he said "time is money." *Time is life.* Ask any elderly person or someone dealing with a degenerative disease. They don't want more money—they want more time. But it's the *quality* of the time you spend at work or at play that really makes you rich.

Resources

In a hurried age when few of us find the time to reflect deeply on the nature of personal freedom and the passage of time itself, Robert Grudin's *Time and the Art of Living* (Ticknor and Fields, 1988) is incredibly refreshing. It can be read one page here and there, or in long, flowing passages that provide mental vacations and insight into balancing work, play, and pleasure.

You can stem the tide of junk mail that engulfs your day by sending a letter or postcard to The Direct Marketing Association (Attn: Consumer Service Dept.), 11 W. 42nd Street, P.O.BOX 3861, Grand Central Station, New York, NY 10163-3861. Simply write, "Please remove the following address from your national data files that service the entire direct marketing industry." Add your name and address and drop it in the mail, You may have to do so a couple of times a year, but it works.

Balancing Personal, Family, and Work Needs

More Americans are living alone than ever before. If you are one of those who doesn't have to zone off a personal office for privacy or adjust your schedule to avoid waking a baby, family issues may not be of importance—yet.

During my twenties, years before working from home was popular, I was married to a terrific woman who helped me establish myself as an international management consultant. Our business was based in a charming cottage that had been converted from an old wrought-iron workshop. The garden was large and private, and we were within a few short blocks of downtown Mill Valley, California. We were together almost all the time and felt sorry for our friends who could only see each other "after work" when they were too tired to enjoy each other's company. So far, so good. After we had lived and worked together almost constantly for six years, utter boredom set in and we wound up getting an amicable divorce. Fortunately we remain friends, and we agree that our marriage might have lasted if we hadn't been quite so blindly devoted to working together all the time.

Some of you may be old enough to remember that classic song phrase from Dan Hicks: "How can I miss you if you won't go away?" If my first wife and I had split our shifts, or taken separate breaks or an occasional separate vacation, we might still be together.

But every couple is different. Remember the Ortaldas? They've been working together successfully for ten years, and even though they have different work habits have managed to make the most of them. Mary uses her mornings to get the kids organized, and Robert knocks off early to start dinner. And, after some trial and error, they found a combination of day care and babysitting that works for everyone—and occasionally involve the grandparents so Robert and Mary can escape on vacations together.

If you plan on working from home with your spouse, decide on your different roles well ahead of time. That way, there will be no resentment or hard feelings down the road. But don't be afraid to take over for each other when necessary, or just for fun. In frontier America, the man chopped wood and the woman cooked the meals—but the husband *knew how* to cook, and the wife *knew how* to chop wood in case the other partner fell ill or had to be away.

Children in the house create a unique joy, but they also pose certain problems. You might feel guilty about shipping them off to day care while you stay at home, yet it might be impossible to get anything done while they are around. Robin Williams, the single mother of three who made a small fortune writing and publishing computer books in her home, not only managed to keep her children out of the way without making them feel rejected, but also avoided the stress of feeling guilty at the same time.

"My house was a mess," she says. "I gave up on housework and concentrated on desktop design jobs and writing my books. I did what women have been doing for ages. But instead of taking in sewing, I took in graphics jobs and did them at home in the wee hours after the kids were asleep." Robin made sure she had a normal daily life with her children. She worked at several different part-time jobs so she'd be there when her kids came home from school. Then the four of them would shop, cook dinner, and eat together. After dinner, the kids read and Robin worked. "We've never had a TV, so my children's concentration skills are excellent—they're readers—and I had uninterrupted quiet to work in my office late at night."

Robin's approach to parenting and working has had a lasting effect on her children, who saw her create her independent life. "They've seen what it takes to get where we are now. They know it wasn't a lottery ticket. It was me, working hard." The benefits are apparent. Scarlett, her daughter, designed the decorative alphabets that begin each section for Robin's latest book, *Jargon: An Informal Guide to Computer Terminology*.

School-age children are one thing, but a baby in the house is something else entirely. "The biggest mistake I made at first," says Elaine de Man, an independent writer and editor, "was assuming that I could make the baby fit into my schedule. When she was very young it wasn't so bad, because she slept most of the time and I could work then. But now that she's six months old, her naps aren't always long enough. When it works, when the baby is quietly sitting in her swing next to my desk, I have to admit it's wonderful and very fulfilling. But when it doesn't work, when she's fussing and crying, it's incredibly frustrating."

Grandmas and grandpas are great. But in spite of any promises they may have made while waiting for the blessed event, they invariably have lives of their own and can't be expected to always accommodate your schedule. So do yourself a favor if there's a baby on the way: make arrangements for an in-home babysitter so you can be free to work and to take breaks conveniently with the little one.

The key to the successful family is to remember the reason you decided to work from home in the first place. Don't short-change your personal life in pursuit of financial success.

First Steps in Planning and Setting Up a New Business

If you have decided to make a complete break from the company or institutional world and are ready to head out on your own, you will have to jump through a few hoops first to make real success possible. None of them are particularly difficult, but they will make you define the business you are in and help you set achievable goals. The first hoop can actually be a lot of fun.

Naming the Baby

If you are a dentist for whom a name like Drills R Us won't quite do, you can use your own name for your business. For some businesses, however, your name may not be enough unless you are already well known. But you might be able to include what you actually do in the business name. For example, Mary Jones Design Associates combines a name and a service.

If you are not going to use your own name, you will need to come up with something short and snappy that will keep your image focused in the minds of your potential customers. The Graphics Barn: World Class Posters is much better than the Art Poster Catalog Mail Order Service. And a name like Golden Gate Graphics Barn will help localize your new service. It gives you roots, especially important for a new business that wants to project an established image.

The word *enterprises* is simply another word for *business*. Unless it adds "music" to your name (see page 67), avoid it. And if your business is computer oriented, resist using *Comp* or *Compu* in the name. It's been done.

Once you think you have it, say the name out loud several times to be sure it isn't a tongue-twister or difficult to pronounce. Test it on others by asking them to say it. And remember that you will have to say it a thousand times when answering the phone.

Since we are a multicultural society, make sure your business name, product name, or service mark doesn't mean something derogatory in another language. When Coca Cola entered the Hong Kong market with their slogan "It's the real thing," it translated into "Bite the wax tadpole." The Japanese version of Kentucky Fried Chicken's "Finger lickin' good" wound up as "Bite your fingers off." One of the most famous blunders was committed by General Motors when they introduced the Chevrolet Nova. After much fanfare, the car received the coolest reception imaginable in Mexico, where "No va" means "Doesn't go." It didn't.

Before you get committed to your new name, do a "prior use" search to make sure you aren't accidentally stealing a name that is already in use in a similar business. Simply call the county clerk in the county where you set up your company, or, if you have launched an incorporated business, call the secretary of state's office in your state. If you plan to go national with your company, contact the registrar of copyrights at the Library of Congress to establish a national trademark or service mark.

When I started out as a management consultant in the late sixties, I used part of the name of my *San Francisco Chronicle* column and called my company The Innerspace Project. It sounds dated now, but in 1968 the idea of putting ecology into business practices and giving workers a more equal voice in management decisions was rather avant-garde. I conducted a name search, discovered no one was using the name, and trademarked it.

The first year I attracted a number of major clients, and success seemed assured. Then I began getting one, two, or three phone calls a day asking if I had any king-size waterbeds available for immediate delivery. As I walked down the streets of the little town where I'd lived for years, people winked and said, "Wow! Waterbeds, huh? You sure know how to make a buck!" This was not good. Here I was, trying to establish myself as a high-level consultant, and someone had apparently come along with a mountain of capital and launched Innerspace Waterbeds. I called them and told them the problem. We met, and over an amiable lunch they showed sympathy for my dilemma, acknowledged that I had trademarked the Innerspace name, and agreed to change their name. But they didn't. It was going to cost at least ten thousand dollars just to start legal proceedings against them. Because our two companies were not competing in the same field, and the names weren't exactly the same, my attorney told me it was unlikely I would win such a lawsuit.

The whole situation later proved to be not much more than an inconvenience, but the moral of the story is to do prior-use research no matter how unique you think your name or logo is. It could save you from the nuisance of phone calls at the very least, and the loss of business at the worst.

There are a number of other reasons to control your company or corporate name, trademark, or service mark. (A service mark is a slogan, such as General Electric's "We bring good things to life.") Once you are successful, you will be able to document your prior use if anyone tries to imitate you in your field. More important, you don't want to be confused with a business whose ethical or quality standards aren't up to yours. And, finally, if you want to sell your business later, ownership of your company name adds real value.

Once you have chosen a name, most states require that you publish a "Doing Business As" (DBA) announcement under "Fictitious Businesses" in the classified section of at least one newspaper in the town or county where your business is based. In addition to your company name, you will have to describe your business and include the street address—in this case, of your home. This may also be required to establish a business bank account; the rules vary from state to state. In California, this advertisement must appear once a week for four weeks. Nevada, on the other hand, doesn't even have the DBA category. Check with your local officials.

business name or names listed herein.
This statement was filed with the County Clerk of Santa Clara County on April 28, 1994
(May 11, 18, 25, June 1, 1994)

Walker&Hale
FICTITIOUS BUSINESS
NAME STATEMENT
File No. 283446
The following individual(s) is (are) doing business as WALKER&HALE, 366 California Ave. Palo Alto, CA 94306.
CUMMINGS WALKER, WANDA HALE
This business is conducted by an individual. Registrant has begun business under the fictitious business name or names listed herein.
This statement was filed with the County Clerk of Santa Clara County on April 25, 1994.
(May 4, 11, 18, 25, 1994

ServiceScan
FICTITIOUS BUSINESS
NAME STATEMENT
File No. 283282

The Mission Statement

Let's invent a small business and call it the MemBrain Company. First we need to define the business and identify our target markets:

> *The MemBrain Company is a computer and software buying and installation service for home-based desktop publishing, mail order, and accounting services.*

Notice that we specified our customer base: desktop publishing, mail order, and accounting services. These are *vertical* markets. If we had said "everybody," it would be harder to focus and to develop a track record within a market. By sticking to selected vertical markets, we will be able to concentrate our marketing efforts and get referrals from people in a core group of businesses who know each other.

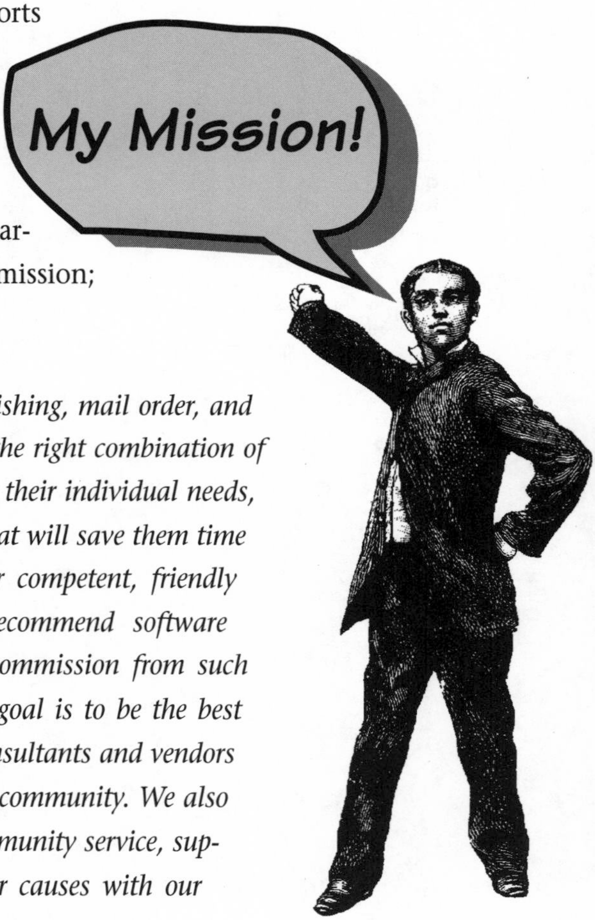

Now that we know who we are targeting, we need to describe our mission; that is, what we will do:

> *We will help desktop publishing, mail order, and accounting services select the right combination of software and hardware for their individual needs, and help them get deals that will save them time and money. We will offer competent, friendly telephone support and recommend software trainers, taking a small commission from such trainers for referrals. Our goal is to be the best local computer systems consultants and vendors to small businesses in our community. We also want to play a role in community service, supporting charities and other causes with our expertise rather than money.*

As you can see, your mission statement doesn't have to be long. The important thing is that it helps you focus on what you are setting out to do. After all, if you don't know where you are going, you aren't likely to get there. The mission statement is your way of navigating.

Once committed to paper, your mission statement can become a talking point with your family, partner, or potential investors. You can refer to it as the basic resource when writing copy for brochures and public-relations pieces such as press releases. You might even post it on your office wall to keep you from wandering too far afield.

An important thing to remember, however, is that your mission statement is not written in stone. You can modify and refine it as your business develops.

Your Job Description

After you have created your mission statement, zoom in on the most important detail in the picture: your job description. Here's one for our mythical hero, Frank Wagstaff.

> *Frank Wagstaff will be MemBrain's consultant - for-hire, designing computer systems for home-based businesses. He will purchase the software and hardware systems, resell them to clients, and install them on site. If training is necessary, he will refer clients to trainers. He will also be MemBrain's account executive, going after new accounts.*

When writing your job description, use your own name. This gives you more objectivity than saying "My Job Description." Write a job description that's appropriate to your skills, but don't set yourself up to wear too many hats. Initially, you might also have to be the sales department, complaint desk, and billing department, but eventually you might hire someone else to take over tasks that are not your main areas of expertise. If you do, check their credentials, and always hire people you like as human beings.

If a partner or spouse will be working with you, get together with them to write their job description as well. Try to assign tasks to the partner who is good at and enjoys them. If one of you likes typing, talking on the telephone, or going to the post office before 9 A.M., assign that person to that job. By sorting these things out as you write your job descriptions during the early formation of your business, you will save a lot of misunderstanding. You can always trade off later for variety or in an emergency, as the pioneers did.

The Business Plan

If you are going to apply for a Small Business Administration loan or seek venture capital, you will need a business plan. Jon Goodman, a University of Southern California business professor, gives students this macabre example of what's required. "A great business plan describes a company in such a way that if you were struck and killed by a truck while walking across the street, a passerby could snatch up your business plan and implement it as well as you could." Your mission statement and job description(s) will help you create your business plan, which contains six basic components:

- A description of your business.
- A description of the products and services your business will be providing.
- An identification of the market for your products or services.
- A description of your operating requirements.
- A list of your projected start-up costs, as well as income statements and monthly cash-flow statements for the first three years.
- A conclusion summarizing your business goals.

It's not as difficult as it may sound. For the most part, you can simply elaborate on your mission statement and job description. Here are a few tips to help you along:

- Describe your product or service as simply yet completely as possible.
- Cite what makes your product or service truly different or better than what's already out there.
- Explain how your product or service is cheaper to deliver or lower in price than the competition.
- Spell out how you have secured any necessary trademarks, service marks, patents, or copyrights.
- Illustrate your market position. If you are part of a new industry, show how. When Federal Express, McDonald's, and Apple Computer were launched, new investors rushed in to the new markets of overnight delivery, fast-food franchising, and personal computing. You may not have such enormous potential, but if there is a developing niche or new market, it can be very sexy to investors.
- Estimate how much money will be needed to start and sustain the business, and what it will be spent on.
- Project the financial results for which you are aiming.

For additional help, you might want to refer to *How to Write a Business Plan* by Mike McKeever, which goes into greater detail on the elements and benefits. Not only does it show you how to pull together all the parts of a plan, it shows you how to refine and use it to get the money you need. You can order it directly from the publisher: Nolo Press, 950 Parker Street, Berkeley, CA 94710.

Your Business and the Law

Among the earliest decisions you will have to make is what type of business ownership should you set up. A sole proprietorship, where the business is owned by one individual, is the most common and simplest form of ownership for a new business, but it exposes you to losing your personal assets if you are sued in the course of doing business. By incorporating, you can sometimes shield your personal property, leaving only corporate assets vulnerable to attachment and sale in case of a judgment against the corporation. However, since even a corporate structure can be judged as a thin shield by the court, you should get professional advice.

Just because you may no longer be receiving a paycheck, don't imagine you will suddenly be able to hide from the IRS. As a small business or independent contractor, you must include your Social Security number on your invoices. No business will even issue you a check without it, since they will have to fill out tax Form 1099 for moneys they have paid you. If you incorporate, get a separate tax ID number from the IRS, and you won't need to give out your Social Security number.

A business license may be required for your business; different cities and counties have different requirements. If you are buying items wholesale and selling them retail, call your state or county auditor's office, city hall, or your local chamber of commerce to determine whether you need a vendor's license. California law, for example, requires that you obtain a resale number from the State Board of Equalization.

Your local Small Business Administration office has a number of publications to assist you, including the *Small Business Directory,* which contains a complete list of publications and video tapes and is included in their Small Business Startup Kit.

Be a Good Neighbor

An important key to creating a successful environment for your enterprise is to make it compatible with your neighborhood. Your neighbors probably won't appreciate a business sign planted on your lawn or posted in your living room window. In some neighborhoods, commercial signs are actually outlawed. If you live in a planned community or own a condo managed by a homeowners' association, review the covenants, conditions, and restrictions (CCRs) to see if and how your business will fit in. In addition to the CCRs, check into local residential zoning laws. They usually allow home-based businesses, but they may not allow a lot of inventory and will probably impose limits on automobile traffic.

Auto repair and light industry (such as metal fabrication) are usually outlawed in residentially zoned neighborhoods, though such regulations may be overlooked in remote rural and unincorporated areas, and some parts of large cities. In any case, check first, since being reported by neighbors or discovered and shut down can be costly in lost business, legal expenses, and court costs. Being a good neighbor to start with is not only good for the community, but it may bring you business and referrals, too.

Resources

The Business Information Center (BIC) of the Small Business Administration (SBA) offers one-on-one counseling with a member of the Service Corps of Retired Executives (SCORE) who can help in developing personalized business plans for small business owners. Currently, SBA BICs are located in Seattle, Houston, Atlanta, St. Louis, and Los

Angeles. The electronic bulletin board system is available twenty-four hours a day, seven days a week at (800) 859-4636 for 2400-baud modems and (800) 697-4636 for 9600-baud modems.

The American Women's Economic Development Corporation (AWED) offers programs that focus on teaching business fundamentals to women, including how to create a solid relationship with a banker, accounting fundamentals, and how to develop peer-group support. Founded nearly twenty years ago, AWED offers intensive business training courses in a number of locations throughout the country. For more information, write to AWED's national headquarters at 71 Vanderbilt Avenue, Suite 230, New York, NY 10169.

10 *Developing a Professional Business Image*

An uncluttered, businesslike image is essential to giving the impression that your business is a real business. Even if it is as enjoyable as a hobby—which working from home certainly can be—don't advertise the fact with amateur graphic design, and don't scrimp on design and printing. Creative care and money invested in your image now will pay off later many times over. With professional-looking business stationery, your correspondents won't know whether you are starting out or long-established.

Letterhead and Business Cards

Your letterhead creates that important first impression, and your business card creates the impression most likely to remain with people after you have left the conference table. They both carry your message to the world, and they must match each other so you can create an identity, a coherent look that everyone will immediately recognize as having come from you—and no one else.

Unfortunately, many business people have no idea how to create a company image on paper. Too many think that if they just futz around with the twenty-four fonts they have on their computer, the right combination will eventually appear. If possible, enlist the services of a professional graphic designer, who will have a more objective and fresher way to project your image into the marketplace.

If you are thinking of using a logo—a picture trademark such as Mobil Oil's flying horse—you really should consider outside design services for the highly specialized skill of creating a logo that is appropriate for you. Consider images you think will represent your business well, from the silhouette of a tree to a three-dimensional image or a photograph.

Alternatively, you can use a logo*type,* such as International Business Machines did with their initials, IBM. A logotype uses the alphabet to create a distinctly recognizable image. Again, consult a professional graphic designer. Your logo or logotype then goes on letterhead and business cards, promotional T-shirts, and on your product. You want to impress your logo into the minds of your audience.

To help people remember you, consider paying a little extra each month to have a phone number that sounds businesslike, such as 555-2000. It's easier for people to remember, and it sounds as though you are on the thirty-third floor of the Megacorp Towers. You can also order a custom number that spells out a name, such as OUR-BOOK. These substitutions are easy to remember but can be difficult to dial, so also show the actual numbers on your business cards, brochures, and letterhead.

After you have settled on your letterhead, envelope, and business card design, try to get at least three printing bids, since quotes may vary by as much as 400 percent. Get one from a mom-and-pop storefront printer, one from a giant printing plant that may be able to gang your materials with another job that uses the same kind of paper and card stock, and one from a medium-sized mail-order printer. Then decide where you will get the most for your money.

Once you have got your printed materials, start networking right away by asking the printer if you can leave a small stack of business cards on the counter. It shows off their work and gives you exposure. Who knows? His next customer might be your next client.

Brochures

If you worked in a corporate setting, you learned to keep your head down. You certainly didn't cruise the hallways telling people what great things you were doing for the organization. But you won't survive independence unless you learn to toot your own horn.

Nothing succeeds solely on its own merits, so you will have to create a certain amount of recognition in the marketplace. This is where a brochure can be a powerful image-builder and door-opener. With a brochure, you can tell your potential clients who you are, what you have done, and for whom you have done it. It's the main component of what will become your sales kit. You can mail it out or leave it behind after a personal visit, so you and your story will be remembered after you leave.

Your brochure can be as simple and inexpensive as a single letterhead-size sheet designed on your computer, printed on a laser printer, and folded to fit into a business envelope. Or it can be a full-color booklet produced at greater expense. If a brochure isn't appropriate for your line of business, you could prepare a single-page biography that includes a list of clients served, projects accomplished, and a capabilities statement. Just remember that any materials you deliver to your prospects must look as good and read as easily as those issued by the "big guys" who are your competition. Don't compromise on this. If you aren't an accomplished writer, hire one. A professional writer can be as important to your success as your lawyer and accountant. Hire a professional graphic designer, too.

The brochure should not only describe the features of your service or product, but the *benefits* a customer will receive by doing business with you. For example, a housecleaning service may have wet/dry vacuums, a wide range of mops and brooms, and a brand new van. Those features are important, but what is far more interesting are the *benefits* the service offers, such as house cleaning without disturbing the daily schedule of the inhabitants and organic cleaning materials that won't pollute the home.

Nothing succeeds on it's own merits, so you will have to create a certain amount of recognition in the marketplace.

Short print runs at a professional print shop let you experiment but drive the per-piece cost up. The economic advantage of a short run, however, is that if one version of your brochure doesn't pull the number of cus-

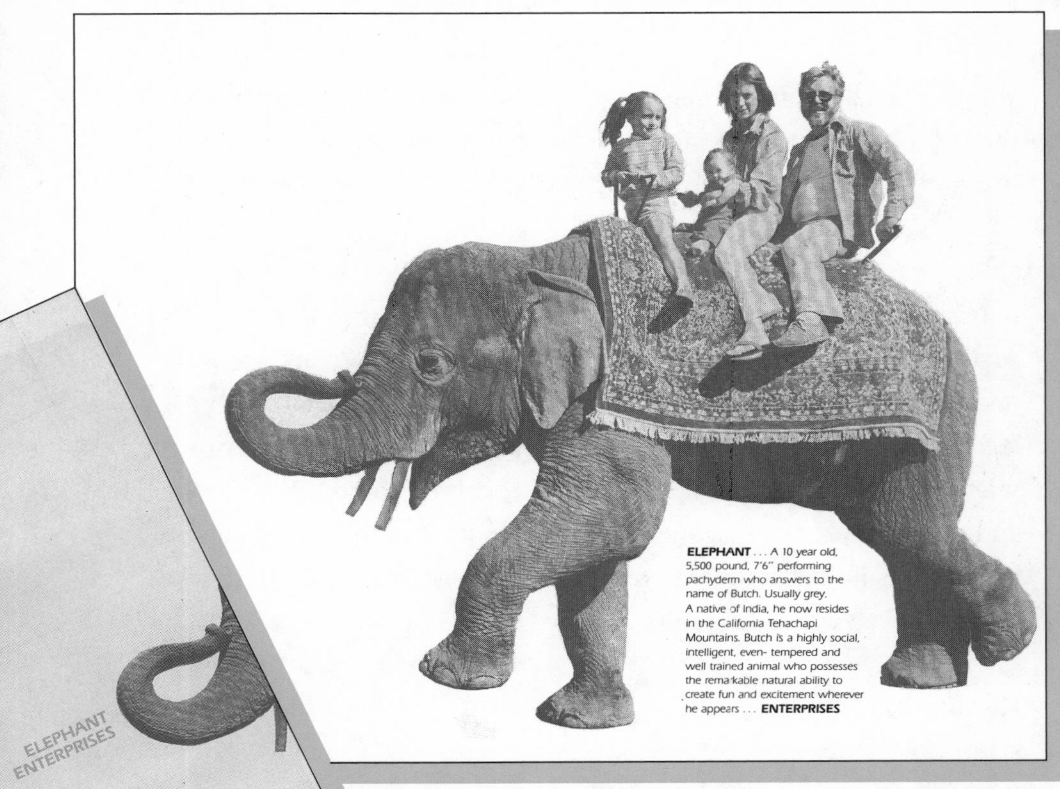

tomers you expected, you can go back to the drawing board and redesign it with a new approach. Once you hit on the right brochure, get a larger quantity printed, since a large print run can be only slightly more expensive than a short one.

If you plan to mail your brochure, you might want to design it as a self-mailer with an attention-grabbing cover on one side and your return address, a headline, and the recipient's address and postage on the other side. Self-mailers don't have to be taken out of an envelope for the headline words and "grabber" pictures to be seen immediately, and they may rivet the attention of your prospects more quickly. An attention-catching design reduces the possibility that your piece will be trashed before your message is even given a chance. On the other hand, if your brochure is sent in a separate envelope, it will be perceived as a classier missive. Because people receive very few personal letters, the more your mailing appears like personal mail, the more it will stand out from the day's barrage of junk mail and the more attention it will receive. Including a postage-paid response card will boost responses considerably.

Once you have a well-written, cleanly designed brochure, you must publish it far and wide. *Publish* simply means to make public, so put a small stack of your brochures on the counter of local copy shops, at restaurants where you are known, or on the free literature table at your local library or bookstore. It can work wonders. If you make personal sales, delivery, or service calls, leave the brochure behind to summarize and reinforce your message. If you are using the telephone to drum up business, mail the brochure to reinforce what you have said and to give your prospects something to keep.

Resources

Paper Direct and Queblo are excellent sources for desktop publishing papers for printing brochures, reports, letterhead, envelopes, business cards, and labels. Many include colorful motifs and designs, so all you have to do is run them through your laser printer to create pieces that look like they cost far more to produce than they actually do. Using these pricey custom papers for long runs, however, would not be cost-effective. Paper Direct, P.O. Box 618, Lyndhurst, NJ 07071-0618. (800) 272-7377; fax, (201) 507-0817. Queblo, 1000 Florida Avenue, Hagerstown, MD 21741. (800) 523-9080; fax, (800) 554-8779.

Mail-order printing companies such as NEBS and DELUXE have a number of generic logos and type styles available for letterhead, invoices, statements, mailing labels, and other forms. For an additional fee, they will use your original logo or logotype. NEBS, 500 Main Street, Groton, MA 01470-9901. (800) 225-6380; fax, (800) 234-4324. DELUXE, P.O. Box 64046, St. Paul, MN 55164-0046. (800) 328-0304.

11 Contact! Finding and Keeping Clients

While you are celebrating the joys of working from home—including the freedom to work around-the-clock or to skip work for entire days—remember that hardly anything ever succeeds solely on its own merits. Running your own business should include consistent job-seeking even when you have current clients or customers. The best way to preserve the pleasures of the independent life is to make it a habit to do something at least every day or two to get out your message. There are lots of ways to communicate the pride and joy you take in providing your product or service. The important thing is to make sure your story is told to the right people, at the right time, and often.

Join business organizations, such as your local chamber of commerce and professional or trade associations specific to your business. Network. Attend meetings and functions and get involved. Let your auto mechanic and your dentist know that you are establishing a home-based business. They will probably want to help by connecting you with potential clients. (If you offer a service you have "clients"; if you sell products you have "customers.") And whenever you hand your business card or brochure to someone, give two. The second

one just may get into the hands of someone looking for somebody exactly like you.

If you are still working close to the corporate world, the best sources of clients and referrals are your colleagues. Signing up your former company as your first account is a great way to start your new venture. Management and former teammates already know what you can do and what you are like to work with. And it's especially attractive for them to still have your talents available without the added costs of benefits. But if you don't have an opportunity like this, there are many things you can do to make your message reach the eyes and ears of the right prospects.

First, make a habit of reading newspapers as though you were looking for a job. But don't hover over the classifieds. Read news stories about reorganizations, product-line announcements, and other indications that businesses need new people and additional services. Find a need and fill it!

Cold Calling

The goal of a cold telephone call is to pleasantly and clearly let potential clients know who you are, what you have done, what you can to do for them, and how they will benefit from your service or product. "Cold" is an unfortunate term that simply means you are calling without an invitation. There should be nothing cold about it.

Try to make your calls on Tuesday, since by then your prospect has gotten Monday out of the way and has set a pace for the week. If you must call on a Monday, do so after lunch. The person who receives your call—if you get past the assistant or the answering machine—will have taken care of a lot of work in the morning and returned from lunch more relaxed. Wednesday isn't good because it's the twilight zone between the first half of the week and the heading-home days of the second half. Thursday is fine, but Friday is the worst day to call since people are already imagining the weekend. But don't let these rules of thumb get in your way if you are truly inspired, especially if the day's news applies to your business and gives you a timely reason to make contact and a current topic to discuss.

If you feel timid about making those all-important calls, think of them simply as "first" calls, ones that start the sales-and-project cycles and long-term relationships. With the proliferation of voice mail and answering machines, you are likely to reach a device rather than a person anyway, which allows you to present yourself with no interruptions. Introduce yourself, leave a message that's short and sweet, and give your name again and your phone number at the end. Close with, "I look forward to hearing from you," or, "Thanks for listening." If you don't hear back within a few days, call back until you get a definite "I'm really not interested." Otherwise, you may be overlooking a prospect who was simply too busy with other matters to respond to you more quickly.

Whether you make your phone calls on Monday mornings only on spring days under the sign of Leo, or only on Thursdays during leap years—one thing is true the year round: If you don't make the calls, you probably won't get the business! No one likes rejection, but the salesperson who hears no the most also hears yes the most. Or, as a character said in one of those colorful Damon Runyon stories, "No horse ever won a race it didn't enter."

There are simple things I do to get the most out of my follow-up calls. I always begin by saying something like, "Bob Hirsch is expecting my call. This is Jeff Berner." I say my name last to spare the receptionist the task of asking, "What did you say your name was?" When Bob gets on the line I will briefly remind him who I am. "This is Jeff Berner, the fellow who wrote the booklet about working from home. You asked me to call today." This puts the ball in his court.

Don't lose heart if you don't succeed the second time. Look confidently toward a future opportunity to make a third or fourth contact after a reasonable period of time. If subsequent calls aren't accepted or your voice mail message isn't returned, don't take it personally. Only about 17 percent of all business phone calls get through to the right person on the first try, including expected calls. Keep trying until you get a definite no. Even though some people say no by ignoring you, you won't know which ones they are unless they finally tell you so.

Elaine de Man found this out during her sixth and what she thought would be her final call to a potential client. She and her partner, aerial photographer Jordan Coonrad, publish a calendar of world-class golf courses as seen from the air, called "Fairways to Heaven." She was trying to sell the calendars in large quantities to companies for use as premium gifts customized with the firm's name. She had about given up on one fellow who never returned her calls, but decided to try him just one more time. When he picked up the phone and heard it was she, he was delighted. "I'm glad you called!" he told her, "I've been carrying your phone number around with me for a couple of weeks, but haven't had a chance to call." He ordered fifteen hundred calendars on the spot, and has since become her biggest customer.

If prospective accounts reply, "Not at this time," ask in a relaxed, conversational way if you may contact them again. If they suggest a time or date, make a commitment: "I'll give you a call during the first week of July." Then, absolutely, positively, call them on the specified date. This not only fulfills the social contract you have made with your prospect; it sets you apart from the hit-or-miss crowd that will just keep trying other numbers if they don't score the first time. You will have performed by doing what you said you would do when you promised to—an increasingly rare quality that is noticed and appreciated.

I have had to wait up to a year or more for some of my own follow-up calls to pay off. In 1988, the marketing director of Okidata asked me if I would be interested in writing and designing a sixteen-page booklet featuring celebrity spokesperson Steve Allen to introduce a new computer printer. I answered that I would be able to jump into the project within a few days. One full year went by before I had a contract, but my enthusiasm never waned. I phoned every few weeks to see how their plans were developing, sent cartoons about the computer industry, and sent occasional faxes. They often replied that we would be working together "in a week or two." After the complex machinery of corporate management clicked to the right combination, the lock opened and I was flown to their New Jersey headquarters to start the job. The first evening, over dinner at a Japanese country inn, I asked their decision-maker why he had chosen me when there were hundreds of similar talents just across the river in Manhattan. He replied that after seeing how my interest in his project never flagged, he knew I would surely be fully dedicated to the project once I got my teeth into it.

Direct Mail

If you have created a brochure, mailing it directly to your prospective clients or customers can be an effective business builder. Unfortunately, the direct-mail industry has learned that you must send approximately seven individual pieces before you will get a response. Follow-up calls to the person to whom you addressed the mailing is essential to making your efforts pay off. Some mailings hit on the first try; others never take hold amid the masses of daily mail we all receive. Statistically, if you get a 3-percent response on a single mailing, you are doing very well.

You can increase your chances enormously by carefully building a mailing list or by purchasing lists from houses that specialize in them. Computerized mailing-list houses will send you a catalog of the lists they maintain, such as people who go camping three times a year or more, or those who buy a lot of photographic supplies. They can rent or sell you a list so finely tuned that you can practically reach all the left-handed women dentists practicing in North Carolina if you need to. The categories are endless, and the lists are regularly updated so you won't be sending material to the dead-letter office. Renting lists isn't cheap, but if you have the right list and the right message, it can be very effective.

If you are computerized, buy a mailing list from a supplier who will supply it on a disk compatible with your computer, and print it out on clear labels with a type face that harmonizes with your stationery. Better yet, print directly on your envelopes with a laser printer, producing the most professional appearance possible. Whatever you do, don't hand-address envelopes unless you are a calligrapher or have clear, professional handwriting such as the kind architects are known for. If your only choice is to purchase lists on pre-printed labels, be sure to see a sample of the printed product first to make sure it won't detract from your image.

Mailing List Houses

Here are just a few of the many mailing-list houses who will rent you a list of people with the exact profile you want to reach with a mailer about your product or service.

Research Projects offers a wide range of lists including art museums, one-partner attorneys in four-person offices, all of America's daily newspapers and their editors' names, hypnotists, and roller-skating rinks, plus lists defined by ethnic, income, and geographic distinctions. Their free catalog will trigger enterprising ideas. Research Projects allows customers to specify the interrelated categories they require to reach any specific market. For example, you might want to reach golf professionals under the age of thirty-five living east of the Mississippi River. Furthermore, if you develop a unique list yourself, Research Projects might rent it from you on a royalty basis. P.O. Box 449, Woodbury, CT 06798. (203) 263-0100; fax, (203) 263-0132.

American Bar Association, 750 N Lake Shore Drive, Chicago, IL 60611. (312) 988-5435. Lists lawyers by specialty, geography, and other factors.

American List Counsel is as broad in scope as Research Projects and is an authorized wholesale representative of other major list compilers such as Dun & Bradstreet. 88 Orchard Road, Princeton, NJ 08540. (800) 252-5478; fax, (201) 874-4433.

Best Mailing Lists, Inc., 34 W 32d Street, New York, NY 10001. (212) 868-1080 or (800) 692-2378; fax (212) 947-0136.

CBS Magazines, 1515 Broadway, New York, NY 10036. (212) 719-6677.

Donnelley Marketing Information Services is one of the largest and oldest list-management firms. 1351 Washington Boulevard, Stamford, CT 06902. (203) 353-7000.

Dun & Bradstreet International Services has had its finger on the American demographic pulse for decades. 99 Church Street, New York, NY 10007. (212) 265-7525.

World Data is a list brokerage and management firm that offers database management services, a newsletter, and a magazine to keep clients fully informed about the direct-marketing world. 5200 Town Center Circle, Boca Raton, FL 33486. (800) 331-8102; fax, (407) 368-8345.

If you are embarking upon a business that requires truly large mailings, you might want to invest in a software system that cleans your mailing list by eliminating duplicate and undeliverable addresses, then prints the addresses directly onto envelopes. It's a good long-term investment for a small business that does a lot of direct-mail marketing.

With your own computer and laser printer, you can harness the infinite power of computer-aided marketing to print a cover letter tailored to each potential client. Let's say you are a consultant in the landscape-gardening business, and a business park you read about in the newspaper is having trouble with deer munching on their shrubbery. In your letter to them, you simply mention that you are especially knowledgeable about ways to encourage deer to eat at some other salad bar. Avoid using the artificial approach—"As you know, *Mr. Frederickson*"—that is so common in junk-mail letters, but do localize your cover letter to your potential client's particular needs.

Time your mailings to the seasons. For example, if your product or service is tied to Christmas, make sure it arrives before December twenty-fifth. And keep in mind that your prospects are more likely to have the money to buy what you are selling before—or quite a bit after—tax time.

The Art of Postage

Tests have shown that postage stamps stimulate better response than metered mail, which practically shouts "junk mail." Furthermore, if you stick the stamp on slightly crooked you will get an even better response. I take the art of postage stamps one step further by using "antique" commemorative stamps that date as far back as 1938 on all my business correspondence. I buy them at or near face value from stamp dealers who advertise in the yellow pages. This assures that my letters stand out in the avalanche of mail and may get opened first.

For example, I will put a 1949 stamp that commemorates the Minnesota Territorial Centennial on a letter to a Minnesotan, and a stamp commemorating the fiftieth anniversary of the trucking industry to a correspondent in the transport business. Since most of these great old stamps are three- and four-cent denominations, I supplement them with modern stamps, but they still stand out. I know they are appreciated because my correspondents often call to let me know how much they enjoy receiving my mail. Some of them even frame the stamps that apply to their profession or give them to their children to start their own collections. These are the details that count.

The Press Release

One of the easiest, least expensive, and most effective ways to raise your profile is to issue a press release. A good press release may make it into the newspapers or inspire an editor to send a reporter out to interview you for a feature story. If newspapers will write about a two-headed calf, they will probably write about you. Good news always appeals to feature editors at newspapers and radio and TV stations across the country, and local papers are constantly looking for stories with a local angle. Don't underestimate the exposure value of neighborhood throw-away shopping-news publications. And don't be afraid to aim high. If you think you have something to offer of national interest, send it to *Newsweek, Entrepreneur,* or any other magazine you think it might fit.

Just about anything can qualify as a news item. You can announce that you are setting up shop, along with the results of the research you did that made you decide to offer your services—say, as a landscape designer. Perhaps you are offering something that has never been seen before in your town. Or you can announce a major project you have just been assigned or recently completed. The idea is to get your name out there as often as possible so people begin to think you are the only landscape designer of note in the whole area.

If newspapers will write about a two-headed calf, they will probably write about you.

Before you or someone you hire writes the release, study the publication you are aiming for to see what section or department your information might fit. Call the paper or magazine for the name of the editor who handles your subject area. Then address the release and a cover letter to him or her. You can even write a number of press releases with different angles aimed at different editors at the same publication.

While just about anything goes for the content of the press release, there are some basic requirements. It should be printed on your letterhead. In the top right corner, type CONTACT: followed by your name and phone number where you can easily be reached, even if it appears on your letterhead. Underneath, type FOR IMMEDIATE RELEASE or FOR RELEASE AFTER and a date. Precede the main body of text by a short headline that sums up the release: "Gardener Launches Garden

Design Service." Double-space the text, use wide margins, and keep it to a single page. If you must go to two pages, type on only one side of each page and type MORE at the bottom of the first. End the release with either ### or –30– centered below the last paragraph.

Put your best efforts into the first sentence, which can make the difference between your press release being read or not. Tell your story in as few words as possible, and finish the first paragraph with the most important information. Use quotes that enhance the information, but avoid superlatives that sound phony, even if they are true: "'This is the most revolutionary business ever launched in Fiddletown!' says Dr. Halliburton Thirstquench." Just tell it straight, and an editor will easily recognize if your story is useful. Whatever you do, don't try to show off your writing skills here, even if you are an accomplished writer. If you have no special talent or time for writing, engage a publicity or public-relations professional. The Public Relations Society of America, at (212) 995-2230, can refer you to someone in your area available for short-term projects.

"I'm Anderson of the Daily Blade," the stranger explained. "I want to get your picture for the paper."

When writing the copy, be honest, direct, and clear. Keep in mind that the editors getting your release receive lots of other press releases and have limited time. The less work the editor has to do rewriting or polishing what you send, the more likely your release will be published. If you do your homework and write well, chances are it will be published verbatim.

If you want to send a photo of yourself, your product, or your home office, hire a professional photographer. Black-and-white prints should be five by seven inches with a glossy finish. Attach a short, informative caption, typed on a separate piece of paper, to the back of the photo. Send color transparencies only if you know a publication prints color, such as a magazine or Sunday newspaper supplement.

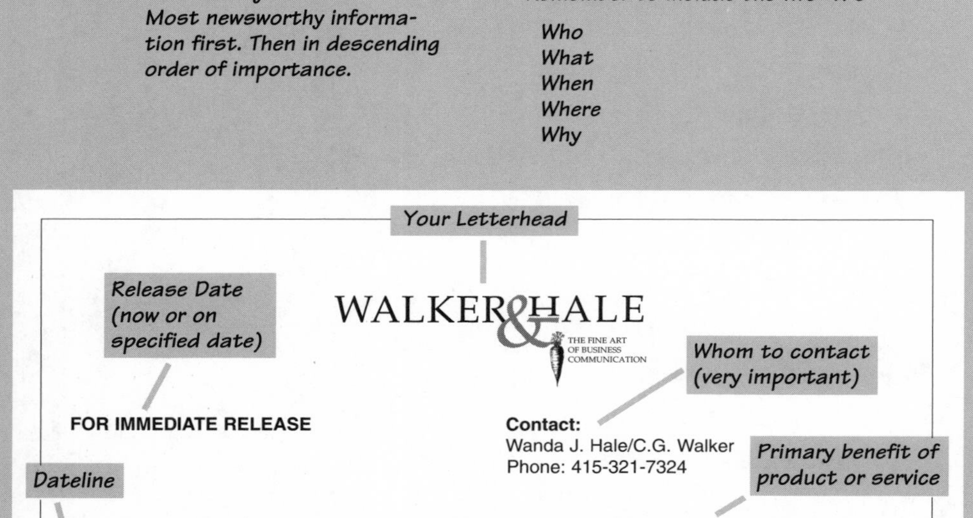

FOR IMMEDIATE RELEASE

Contact:
Wanda J. Hale/C.G. Walker
Phone: 415-321-7324

W & H LAUNCHES PROGRAM TO PROMOTE THE SUCCESS OF HOME-BASED BUSINESSES

PALO ALTO, CA . . . The benefits of high-impact marketing communications are now available to home-based, entrepreneurial businesses in a very cost-effective manner. Walker & Hale — an award-winning marketing design firm — is offering its extensive experience and services to this rapidly expanding segment of the American economy on an interactive consulting basis.

Through a synergistic process, clients themselves implement many if not all aspects of a promotional program formulated through personalized consultation and critiques offered by Walker & Hale. In this way, a "start-up" can gradually put a long-range marketing strategy into action as financial resources become available.

"Hewlett-Packard, Apple Computer, and The Grateful Dead all started in someone's garage," said partner Wanda J. Hale. "Our extensive background in advertising, public relations and marketing graphics can give a start-up company just the edge it needs at affordable rates. Many of the most successful promotional campaigns have been done on a shoestring. Thorough analysis, careful planning and a lot of creativity are the key factors. We see an opportunity to grow with this dynamic marketplace."

A recent survey in the Wall Street Journal confirms that the number of businesses headquartered at home throughout the United States exceeds the total population of California. Often, effective marketing communications are not implemented early on in the business

Remember, this is free advertising. You will have no control over if and when it appears. You will know you have made it into print when your phone starts ringing with inquiries or congratulations. If you don't make headlines right away, don't think for a moment that you have failed. Don't call the paper. Just wait a few weeks and try again with something new.

When you do make it into the pages of a magazine or newspaper, buy as many copies as you can and include the article in your portfolio as a record of your public image.

Television and Radio

Copies of articles about you, along with a press release, photo, and business card, constitute a press kit. This is a good thing to have on hand in case a newspaper or magazine asks for one, and is also a great way to introduce yourself to your local radio or TV station. Noel Coward had a great attitude toward television. "Time has convinced me of one thing," he said, "Television is for appearing on—not for looking at." Appearing on a talk show or newscast can make a big difference in your business or career, and it can be a lot of fun. Don't be afraid to give the national shows a try either, such as "Good Morning, America!" The worst that can happen is that they will pass. Simply call your local stations or the networks, ask who handles guest bookings, and ship them your press kit.

If you do appear on television, ask for a videocassette of your appearance. If you place your order on the same day you appear in the studio, it will be easier for them to locate the footage. Or you could arrange to have a friend tape your appearance with a VCR. Tape any radio or live appearances as well.

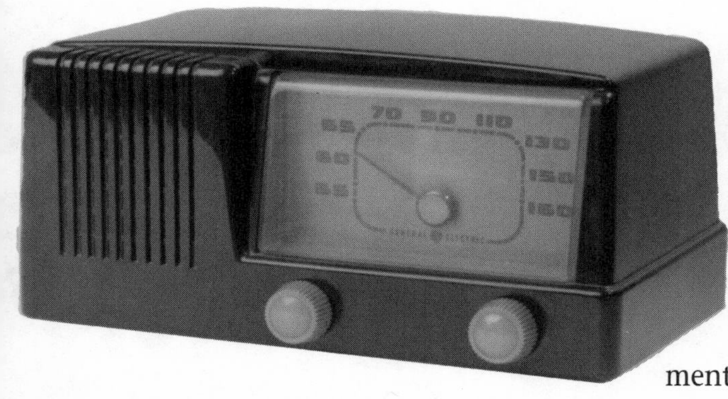

Your sound and videotapes will come in handy later when you solicit lecture bureaus, service clubs, or trade associations for speaking engagements. You can also use them to analyze your presentation by looking into the "living mirror" of videotape to improve your next appearance. I learned this the hard way a few years ago when I appeared on a half-hour interview and call-in television show. I felt relaxed during the broadcast, but when I received the videotape a week later, to my shock, I saw myself blinking constantly. It made me look nervous and uncertain even though I was discussing subjects I felt very confident about. The problem was the combination of bright lights and dry eyes. Now I use eye drops before I appear in front of an audience.

Public Speaking

Another way to get prospective clients to beat a path to your door is to speak before professional associations. Speaking makes you an authority in the eyes of the audience, and it provides you with an opportunity to exchange business cards and establish lasting contacts. A good way to introduce yourself and garner an invitation to speak is to send out a press release.

Over the past twenty-five years I have spoken before many groups, often at no charge. But the exposure brings me a number of challenging and sometimes lucrative offers each year. A photographer I know occasionally gives free slide shows and talks at service clubs and professional groups. As a result, when they need to hire a photographer, they usually think of him. He estimates that these customers account for nearly 20 percent of his income.

Unfortunately, public speaking ranks among America's ten worst fears—just ahead of going to the dentist. If you are a beginner in the speaking arts, practice with a small group of family and friends. Put your main topics in large print on index cards in the order you want to bring them up, and use them as cue cards.

If you want to be a more confident speaker, contact the American Platform Society or Toastmasters International. Both have chapters in many cities throughout the nation and offer workshops that will help you develop your speaking skills. Once you are in front of a real audience, remember that the audience is there because they want to hear what you have to say. They aren't expecting an actor, but a real person who can inform and empower them. They are on your side. Winston Churchill, considered one of this century's great orators, overcame his own terror of speaking by taking a moment before his speech, smiling at the audience, and then using simple language and a personal tone as though speaking to just one person. He never began his talks with a joke, but rather reserved humor as a surprise for later on. He also reminded would-be speakers that a speech must be geared to the ear. Churchill, by the way, had a speech impediment. It didn't stop him for one second. His charisma was legendary.

Newsletters

Important as the media and public appearances are, you don't have to depend upon them. One good and possibly profitable way to develop a consistent vehicle for self-promotion and public relations is to publish your own newsletter. It should contain news and useful information about you and your product or service, and it should have plenty of space to feature one or more of your customers' stories. It should also carry information about your industry or profession, which allows your current and prospective customers know that you are actively keeping abreast of things.

A four-page newsletter four times a year can do the job for most small enterprises. If you aren't an experienced writer, enlist someone to write your newsletter on a schedule that releases an issue with each of the seasons pertinent to your business. Have a professional design the first issue in a page-layout software program (such as PageMaker or QuarkXPress) and supply you with a template you can use for subsequent issues. Print the newsletter on your own laser printer, or have it printed in a walk-in copy shop. Then send it in an envelope (don't forget to use real postage stamps) so it won't arrive bent, torn, or looking like junk mail.

If done right, your newsletter may eventually grow into a profit center. Though most newsletters are sent free, some subscribers are willing to pay for specialized information. Pricier ones usually contain confidential research that is costly to develop, are supported by a very small subscriber base, and may cost $295 or more for four issues.

Barbara Brabec, who has been publishing the *Self-Employment Survival Letter* quarterly for more than a decade, says that the only way to start a successful paid subscription publication is to build a strong local base for a year or two. Then, either continue keeping the subscriber base solidly focused on local businesses, or expand geographically in increments. Casting a wide net to reach a national audience can cost a great deal of money and time.

Advertising

For most home-based businesses, the phone calls, brochures, press releases, newsletters, and other promotional vehicles we have looked at work quite well. However, if you also have a budget for paid advertising, consider the investment with care. Unless you are thoroughly knowledgeable about advertising, carefully select and hire experienced writers, creative talent, and media-placement experts. It takes a real pro to create and place effective ads—and even the pros sometimes drop a coin down a well and don't hear a splash!

The world of print, radio, television, billboard, and other advertising has become so frenetic that it frequently requires the kind of money few home-based businesses can risk to stand out in the crowd. In recent years many smaller companies have shifted much of their advertising budgets into public relations by sponsoring charitable activities, concerts, festivals, golf tournaments, and other activities that bring them not only attention, but appreciation and good will. In a noisy marketplace, it sometimes pays to whisper rather than shout.

On the positive side, with a healthy budget you can hire an ad agency that will design your entire identity—from the name of your business to the look of your publications, invoices, and forms—and then launch your image before the public. The best agencies that provide this kind of corporate design program will involve you in the process, just as your tailor does when making a suit. One size doesn't fit all.

Ensuring Repeat Business

For a moment, let's assume you already have an established base of, say, eight clients. Don't neglect them! After all, no one is more likely to use your services again than someone already impressed by a successful project you have accomplished together. Drop a note or call occasionally to check in. Mail an occasional cartoon about their favorite sports or arts interests, or an article you know will be useful or amusing. This kind of added value and genuine thoughtfulness has become rare these days and will be remembered.

Be bold, have fun, and use a little ingenuity. Herlinda Lopez, a graphic designer in Sonoma County, California, had built a client base of forty restaurants, shops, and other enterprises for her one-person business, MacAccess. Although her clients liked her work, she waited and waited for their repeat business. Then it dawned on her that she could remind those clients about her services and build good will by getting them all together for a barbecue. Herlinda had already developed a small mailing list of people familiar with her talents and straightforward business ethics. It was there on her computer, ready to refresh her presence in the community. Showcasing her talents once again, she designed a terrific invitation to the "First Annual Thank-You Barbecue" and mailed it to her clients with a postage-paid response card. She enlisted one of them, a restaurant, to cater her barbecue in exchange for designing a new menu for them.

Be bold, have fun, and use a little ingenuity.

Twenty-three clients returned their cards and about fifty people attended the party. They all had a wonderful time and were delighted to be appreciated in such a tangible, social way. The barbecue gave Herlinda a comfortable atmosphere in which to engage in shop talk and subtly remind her clients of her services. Two existing clients asked her to meet with them the following week and she was given numerous leads. One lead brought her a client who signed her up to layout and design a program for the local symphony, and that project turned into a year-round assignment.

If you do something similar for your own clients, consider inviting a local newspaper to cover the event as a human interest story, or send them a press release about ten days ahead. It's fine publicity and can often be more effective than paid advertising.

Continued Success

As you succeed in reaching clients and customers and start to bring in business, there are a few things that you should do constantly, consistently, and in an organized way.

First, keep a list of the names, addresses, and phone numbers of everyone you have ever contacted about business, and keep it up to date. Flag those who have become clients, and include notes about their special business interests, hobbies, professional affiliations, family names, and birthdays. Include those who refused your first or even subsequent offers; unless they told you not to call again, they still count as potential business. Collect and store business cards in transparent card organizers. Leaf through them now and then and call a few prospects. You may be surprised to hear, "I was just thinking of you a few minutes ago," and that the timing is right for a new project or a new order.

Second, actively accumulate laurels to emphasize your expertise. If your profession or business turns out a product such as graphic design, photography, copywriting, or advertising, include examples in a portfolio to show potential customers your accomplishments. If your product is three-dimensional, such as pottery or jewelry, and can't fit conveniently into a zippered portfolio, take photographs and create an album. It will impress prospects and give you "trophies" of your efforts beyond a growing bank account.

And finally, remember that you can never afford to postpone seeking new business. If you do, you will go from rags to riches and back many times. I used to wait until I finished one project before looking for another, and my cash flow would come to a screeching halt, sometimes for weeks on end. Don't make the same mistake. Make it a habit to call a few prospective clients each week. Send out a few brochures with cover letters. And follow them up with phone calls and visits. Remember: perseverance equals success.

Resources

If you are one of the thousands of executives and middle-level managers suddenly out of work, consider marketing your particular skills by starting your own consulting service. *Selling Your Services: Proven Strategies for Getting Clients to Hire You or Your Firm* by Robert W. Bly (Henry Holt & Co., 1990) is a valuable resource. Bly, a veteran copywriter and author, provides upbeat, practical tips for anyone trying to sell their services.

Great Connections: Small Talk and Networking for Businesspeople, by Ann Baber and Lynne Waymon, includes tips and techniques to help you move comfortably and professionally from the first hello to the last good-bye. It tells you how to generate business leads, build long-term relationships, and get the most out of conventions and professional meetings. Exercises and quizzes are included to help you build confidence and check your expertise. Available from Waymon & Associates, 622 Ritchie Avenue, Silver Spring, MD 20910. (301) 589-8633.

To reach markets beyond your hometown, get the current annual edition of *The Corporate Address Book: The Complete Directory to Who's Who and What's What in American Business Today* (Perigee Books, Putnam Publishing Group, New York).

If you plan to use direct-mail marketing, see *Secrets of Successful Direct Mail* (NTC Publishing, 1993) by Richard V. Benson, a direct-mail consultant and advisor to Ogilvy & Mather, R.L. Polk, and others. Benson has used direct mail to market practically everything: tours and travel clubs; memberships and magazines; cookbooks and collectors' plates. He shares insights and secrets gained as an agency principal and consultant to *American Heritage and Time-Life*. From VGM Career Horizons, 4255 West Touhy Avenue, Lincolnwood, IL 60646-1975. (708) 679-5500.

If you plan on writing your own press releases, the *Media How-To Handbook* will give you lots of help. It's available from the San Francisco Media Alliance for about six dollars. Media Alliance, Building D, Fort Mason, San Francisco, CA 94123.

If you want to attract nationwide invitations to speak, consider getting a listing in *The Yearbook of Experts, Authorities and Spokespersons* (also known as The Talk Show Guest Directory). For information write to Broadcast Interview Source, 2233 Wisconsin Avenue, Washington, DC 20007. (202) 333-4904.

12 *Making Money and Getting Paid*

Without an organization behind you or a predictable salary to depend on for taking care of monthly expenses, you could end up in a constant state of worry. It can be difficult to budget your resources and save regularly for unanticipated expenses—including the expenses that come with sudden success! Small businesses can fail early on because of a swamp of orders and a lack of production money or personnel to serve demand.

Don't sell yourself short. Call around and get estimates from businesses like yours to find out what your competition charges. That way your prices won't be unreasonably high or so low that your perceived value is low too. No one will want to do business with someone who offers "fire sale" prices before there's a fire. But it's fairly standard practice to bid a little high, giving you room to negotiate and offer a discount to land a contract.

Most consultants to small business recommend having a full year's capital on hand before launching the business. How you accumulate or raise such short-term capital depends on how much you can save, raise from your family, or get from outside investors. On the other hand, don't get too far out on a financial limb or you will be inviting unbearable stress, unreasonable risk, and a guarantee that you won't be making a life but just chasing coins. If you are currently employed, make the transition slowly, with a real plan, and stick to it.

A double whammy is in store for you if your new business is a service. Banks almost never loan money to people who earn their income by signing performance contracts, agreements that specify the client's requirements and your promise to perform certain services by certain dates. If your only collateral is the promise that you will write a software manual or design an advanced hiking boot, you will have a hard time raising capital. The bank might lend money to the boot maker who owns the machinery that makes the boots, because the machinery and the boots have cash value. But the only way they are likely to finance your dream is if you have real estate or other collateral.

Once you are on your own, you may be surprised at how difficult it can be to get paid, particularly if you used to work for a company with its own accounts receivable and legal departments. Unfortunately, larger companies often take advantage of the fact that independent suppliers are grateful just to do business with them and often put small business-

Find Out Anyone's Credit Rating

Office Depot offers individual business credit reports from TRW for about thirty dollars each, which can help you identify risky businesses. You can contact them in three ways:

- To have the service billed to your phone, dial (900) 288-4258.
- To pay with a credit card, dial (800) 488-5775 and touch 1.
- To order free CREDITPRO PC software that will let you retrieve credit reports in minutes by computer and modem, dial (800) 488-5775 and touch 4.

Other major credit-rating firms charge a fee for each request. They include:

- Computer Science Corporation Credit Services, 652 Northbelt, Suite 133, Houston, TX 77060. (713) 878-4840.
- Equifax, 1600 Peachtree Street NW, Atlanta, GA 30309. (404) 885-8000.
- Trans Union Credit Information Company, 555 W Adams Boulevard, Chicago, IL 60661. (312) 258-1717.
- TRW Information Services Division, 505 City Parkway W, Orange, CA 92668. (714) 385-7000.

es at the bottom of their payables list. But there are a few things you can do to reduce your vulnerability.

First, obtain a credit rating for your new account before you go to work or deliver goods. Asking around about their reputation is easy in a small town, but getting the big picture may still be necessary if a lot of money is at stake.

Whether you are offering a service or a product, do everything by invoice to leave a paper trail for you to follow in case of a dispute. The IRS likes that, too. It's also a good idea never to let any account owe you more than you can recover in small claims court. In California, for example, the limit is five thousand dollars.

If you are selling a service, ask your clients to sign an agreement that specifies payment in three parts: a 33-percent advance payment upon agreement, a 33-percent progress payment, and 34-percent payment upon completion or final approval. The advance is the good-faith money your client pays when you both sign a contract or letter of agreement. Once you have delivered the first part of the work, you receive the progress payment and carry on with the project. Your agreement should spell out what portion of the work this entails and the date it is due. The word *progress* takes some pain out of the payment for your client and helps you keep your eye on the calendar. The completion payment is due when you have satisfactorily completed the project.

Small-ticket jobs can be set up with just two payments of 50 percent each, and larger projects can be broken into any number of parts, such as five 20-percent payments. Negotiate a payment schedule that is comfortable for both parties. Doing any work at all without at least a 20-percent advance isn't wise, since you are subsidizing your client until you are paid. In the event that the project goes up in smoke, at least some of your expenses and time will have been paid for. If your client is notorious for slow payment, build in a 1.5-percent-per-month late fee. You can even charge slow payers a slightly higher price for the anticipated nuisance. Some larger corporations aren't yet willing to pay advances, but as they hire more and more independent contractors they will learn to accommodate our needs.

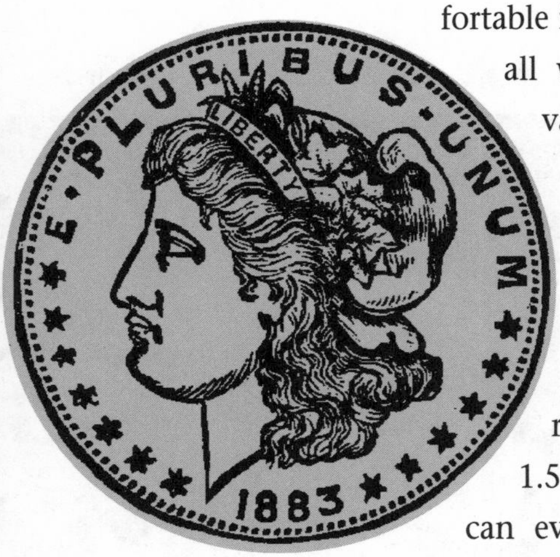

If you are selling a product, ask for a signed purchase order specifying that the goods you deliver are to be paid for within a certain time, say thirty, sixty, or ninety days from delivery. You can also negotiate the terms. For example, a customer could ask to pay the first half of the bill within thirty days and the balance within ninety days. You can offer a small discount, such as 2 percent, for payment upon delivery. In any case, stipulate that interest of 1.5 percent per month will be charged on overdue balances.

If you have a product and are just starting out, consigning your wares may be the only way to get your merchandise into a particular shop or retail chain. If so, get signed receipts for all your merchandise and agreed-upon conditions for return. You can specify, for example, that if the goods haven't been sold within ninety days, the shop must return them to you in salable condition. If they sell, the shop must pay you within a certain number of days of the sale. Learn and follow the payment traditions for your type of business.

Even if business is booming and you have clear, written payment agreements and great relationships with your customers, you can never be certain they will pay on time or be in business long enough to pay you at all. Holidays, the weather, and many other factors can also slow down your cash flow. Desperation can be deadly. Other people may not want to do business with you if you are struggling to keep the phone connected.

Protect yourself against dry spells by building a savings account to cushion you from the effects of uncertain economic conditions, and put money into the account as often as possible. Turn it into a game, if necessary, to add entertainment interest to your savings. For example, you can bet with your spouse on everything from the weather to who will show up at the family picnic. You might say, "I bet fifty dollars the 49ers trounce the Cowboys." If your partner goes for it and the Cowboys win, you deposit fifty dollars into your joint savings account and add to your hedge against taxes, rainy-day business expenses, and retirement.

Rich, poor, or in between, we all need money. If money makes your eyes brighten more than sunrise on a tropical island, then by all means use it as a score-keeping device. But remember, it's just one element in an equation that also includes the amount of leisure time your work earns you and the amount of money you can set aside for your heirs and contribute to worthy causes. You will find that setting a dollar amount on success is a rather shallow way to keep score. You probably know people whose primary goal is money—and you have probably noticed that no matter how much they have, it never seems to satisfy them.

A better benchmark for your success is customer satisfaction. But when all is said and done, your wealth will be measured by the friends you have and the contributions you have made to their success. Your happiness—and that of your family—will give you an enduring sense of accomplishment far beyond pots of gold.

Resource

How to Live Within Your Means and Still Finance Your Dreams, by Robert Ortalda (Fireside Books, 1990), is full of wisdom and contains exercises that can help you develop a practical approach to your business and your life. Ortalda has advised many entrepreneurs and small businesses, and he practices what he preaches.

Running With the Big Dogs: The Vulnerabilities of Being Independent

Working solo, or even with a partner, can make you feel vulnerable in a world of big government and big business and in an ever-changing business climate. Let's look at some of these potential problems and how to deal with them.

You Are a Professional

Without a receptionist in a marble-floored foyer, it might be difficult for other professionals to take you seriously. You will have to convince them. For starters, avoid referring to yourself as a "freelance" anything. The expression dates from the Middle Ages when legitimate warriors swore allegiance to a king or lord, and the rest were roving soldiers and mercenaries who offered the service of their swords and lances to the highest bidder. They were known as "free-lance" soldiers. The term was popularized in Sir Walter Scott's 1819 novel, *Ivanhoe*. Because 90 percent of today's working population has sworn allegiance to a company, *freelance* is often interpreted as a code word for "unemployed" or "between jobs."

Instead, refer to yourself as an independent contractor, independent designer, independent writer, or the like. You can call yourself a consultant, though that term was a bit suspect until a few years ago when it became fashionable. "The definition of a consultant," the joke went, "is a guy from out of town." Fortunately, consultants generate more respect today. Another way to sound more solid is to call yourself not just Bill Brelet, but Bill Brelet Associates. Then you can introduce yourself by saying, "I own the Bill Brelet Associates. We specialize in public relations for solo professionals."

Assure your potential clients that even though you are an independent contractor, you are a team player. Let them know that you work with numerous accounts throughout the year, demonstrating that you know how to join and successfully adjust to new groups. Explain that your experience playing "pick-up basketball" makes you even more likely to be an enthusiastic player.

And what about your track record? Even if you are just starting out in your home-based enterprise, you aren't just starting out in life. Saying, "Serving discriminating clients since 1994" won't impress anyone. Instead, point to your experience working in a field related to your new business. Someone who loves cooking, for example, and has done so with distinction for family and friends, can start a catering service and honestly say he or she has been cooking gourmet meals since 1978. If your prospects still resist you because of your short or non-existent track record, offer your service or product with an absolute guarantee of satisfaction. Long-established businesses often do this to land a contract. If you truly lack experience, consider getting a full- or part-time job in the business you want to establish. You will not only learn the ropes and enhance your existing skills, but you will have something to add to your biography when you do launch your enterprise. And you will have made valuable contacts in the field.

Working with Clients

Even though most people report that being their own boss is the number-one joy of working from home, you will actually have many bosses throughout the year as you take orders, fulfill contracts, deliver services, and cater to those who hold a big part of your success in their hands. Sometimes they will act as though they are doing you a favor taking your call or doing business with you. And they are. But don't enter these relationships feeling that everyone has you at their mercy. Go into every meeting in the spirit of being on a team with others who have a common goal—not to win or lose, but to work together on a successful project.

There are all kinds of management styles and personalities. If you run into people with bad attitudes, take the high ground and be patient, knowing that in cases of rudeness, abruptness, and even arrogant politeness *you are not the target.* As long as you do your part to hold up the social contract of clear communication, fair business dealings, and conscientious service, accept grumpiness, forgetfulness, and unreturned phone calls as part of the atmosphere in uncertain times. Remember, you are making a life, not merely a living.

Take the high ground and be patient

On the other hand, you shouldn't put up with excessive guff. I was recently invited to work with a small ad agency to write a newspaper and radio campaign for a local savings and loan. After our first meeting, I woke up at three in the morning after dreaming of some inspired, original copy. Three days later, way ahead of deadline, I went in to present my proposed copy and numerous alternative themes. Two art directors were waiting for me. The head of the agency entered the conference room without so much as a "good morning," listened to my six proposed slogans with a sour face, and then grumbled, "Where are the words 'Grand Opening'?" I then presented a fifteen-second radio spot, while he stared at the table. It was obvious that I wouldn't be able to please him if I danced on the table with Liza Minnelli. So I cheerfully thanked him and his creative team for the opportunity and left to go have a nice day. There are moments in everyone's business life when you just have to ride off into the sunset.

Building Your Staff

If you are a one-man or one-woman band running your own business, you must wear many hats. Even if you know how to perform the many roles that apply to your business, try to resist doing them all unless you want your business to become your whole life. Sometimes it pays to hire outside services to relieve you from drudgery such as typing, accounting, and other tasks that can wear you down. If your space, temperament, and cash flow allow it, you may want to hire an employee. Doing so will add interest to your daily routine. It will also allow you to train someone to take over if you become ill or want to run off to a tropical island for a while. If you decide to hire someone, even part time, research the social security and other tax implications first.

When choosing someone to hire or selecting an outside resource such as an accountant or tax attorney, find someone who will respond to being treated as a team member and with whom you have a mutual goal. Make sure they really appreciate what your enterprise is about. You will then be developing a long-term relationship with someone you can trust and who may send business your way.

Do business with people who do business with you. If you are a home-products distributor and need secretarial services, see if one of your own customers does such work from home. If they are qualified, use them. This way, you will both have a sense of mutuality beyond the exchange of money and services. You might even barter, trading products and services.

Hiring other small independents can free you to do what you do best, while helping you grow a talent pool you can depend on for mutual support and friendship. Your outside support services will inevitably include a large company, such as a full-color printing plant. When you use such firms, don't be just a customer. If your product or service might be useful to them, let them know more about what *you* do. Printers sometimes need graphic designers or photographers, and they certainly have customers who need those services.

Last but not least, don't forget to plan for success! Assume that your home-based enterprise will have all the right ingredients: a terrific product or service, a suitable space, enough money to keep going, good marketing results, and time managed well enough to support your enjoyment of family and friends. Plan in advance how to escape from your home-based independence long enough to be free away from it, too, on well-earned vacations. Train a trusted family member, neighbor, or friend to answer the phone, feed the cat, and fill in while you visit the Lazy JB Ranch in the Rockies or snorkel in Hawaii.

14 *Selecting the Right Equipment*

Back in 1931, when typefaces were still hand wrought, the master type designer Eric Gill wrote that "the introduction of mechanical methods into small workshops has an immediate effect on the workmen. Inevitably they tend to take more interest in the machine and less in the work."

It's as true now as it was then. You will see a bewildering array of ads for "home office" gear. But if you buy lots of nifty-looking equipment before you need it, you will quickly become the tool of your tools. Don't load up with a heap of software packages as tall as the stack the Charlie Chaplin imitator balanced in TV ads during the mid-1980s. Start simple and keep it simple so that you can take advantage of the flexibility and freedom that home office life affords.

Before we look at how to select items to equip what futurist author Alvin Toffler calls "the electronic cottage," lets look at some of the simpler, but equally important, equipment.

The Chair

Mark Twain wrote most of his books in bed, propped up by goose-down pillows. You, on the other hand, will want to start with the best chair you can afford. I am constantly amazed by people who invest a fortune in computers, fax machines, and other sophisticated components, but spend only fifty-nine dollars for the chair they sit on for most of their waking hours. Next to a door that closes, the chair is the most important piece of home office equipment.

The best chairs are fully adjustable and can be positioned from completely upright to almost fully reclined, supporting the great variety of body postures you may take throughout the day.

Before you buy, test drive the chair by sitting in it for a while. Move in it as though answering a phone, typing at a keyboard, or talking with someone across the desk. Make sure it can be adjusted and readjusted easily, so you can give your back and legs different positions during the day. Check that height adjustments are easy to make. The front of the seat should not press against the back of your thighs, or circulation to your legs will be restricted and they will fall asleep. And be sure your chair has a five-pointed star base—which is the most stable—with casters. Once you find the right chair, get a guarantee for a three-day trial period.

For writing with my laptop computer, I use a recliner. I can semi-recline at various heights and angles and write for hours, only minimally aware of my body. At my desk I prefer an armless chair so I can swing around freely without banging into the desk.

Phones

The wide range of telephone services offered by many local companies will enhance even the most low-tech telephone. *Call return* redials the last call you received, whether or not you answered it. *Priority ringing* gives a distinct ring when you get a call from up to ten phone numbers that you preselect. *Call screen* blocks calls from up to ten numbers that you select. *Call forwarding, busy call forwarding* and *delayed call forwarding,* automatically forward phone calls to any number you preselect. Then there is *call waiting,* which often causes more irritation than it's worth. Imagine conducting business with a clerk in a store who says, "Oh, excuse me. Can you step aside a moment? There's someone *behind* you!"

Ideally, you will have a business line and a separate private line installed in your office. If so, a two-line phone will be extremely useful. Line-status lights show you whether each line is ringing, busy, or on hold. Two phone lines are vital if you will frequently be using a facsimile machine or online services such as electronic mail. You don't want to tie up your regular line with data transmissions and miss important calls.

A high-quality, noise-free cordless phone is perfect for a home office because of the freedom it gives you to roam around gathering reference material while you are talking, and to receive calls while you are at the back fence talking with the neighbors or in the kitchen making lunch. Keep in mind, though, that most cordless phones are vulnerable to eavesdropping, since anyone can listen in from just outside your home with equipment available at most electronics stores. If you are concerned about this, consider one of the high-end models that digitally encodes and transmits messages to provide security.

If you are at your computer keyboard a lot, a lightweight telephone headset will let you continue working without losing the use of a hand or crooking your neck and shoulder to hold a handset to your ear. Cordless models are a distinct advantage because they allow you to jump up to answer the door without ripping your equipment out of the wall. A speakerphone will also allow you to roam your office talking hands-free, but many people find the hollow sound heard at the other end obnoxious.

Cellular phones, popularly known as car phones, are useful for sales reps, doctors, building contractors, and others who are on the road a lot. Pocket-size portable phones that can be plugged into an automobile cigarette lighter or a pocket battery pack are especially useful for reps taking an order in the field or distributors who want to call in new orders or make appointments on the go. Like cordless home phones, cellular phones make your conversations vulnerable to eavesdropping. Affordable "scrambler" systems are available, and when digital technology becomes the telephonic norm, conversations will be universally secure. Cellular reception varies depending on the terrain. If you will be using a cellular phone in an essentially flat city such as Phoenix, a low-end model will serve you well. But in a mountainous area, or downtown surrounded by high-rise buildings, you will need a more powerful model. At the very high end, there are satellite services that can keep you in touch in Timbuktu.

Be sure you need a cellular phone before investing, because service is expensive—you are charged for receiving calls as well as making them.

Read the contract carefully before signing on the dotted line. Many have minimum-usage levels, some charge a penalty for early termination of the contract, and some have automatic renewals.

If a cellular phone isn't in your budget but you like the idea of having freedom from your house phone, consider getting a pager. A pager accepts phone calls wherever you are and displays the caller's phone number on a small screen. Then it's up to you to return the call.

Whether you choose a cellular phone or a pager, you will be liberated from the house arrest some solo home-based workers impose on themselves while waiting for calls. Get out on your bike, take a walk, or drive to the beach. Be free *and* in touch.

Answering Systems

I once dreamt that a solo home worker, lost in trying to sound like a large company, answered his phone with, "How may I direct your call? To my left ear or to my right?" That was a dream. A nightmare is when an untrained family member grabs the phone when you are outside watering the roses. Make sure that no one answers your business line unless they will answer and take your messages as professionally and cheerfully as you do.

How well you or your phone helper answers your calls can make a tremendous difference since it may be the first impression people get about who you are and how professional your business is. Avoid answering with an imitation of the rote verbiage the phone-bank slaves at large corporations must use: "Thank you for calling the Graphics Barn. How may I help you?"

Yours is a small business run by a real person. The luxury of sounding human and personally available won't lose you business; on the contrary, people will be happy to find someone who isn't a robot and who has time for them. My company is Jeff Berner Creative Services, and for many years I have answered my own telephone. I say simply, "Jeff Berner."

Answering "live" is the best way to remain available to clients and customers. On the other hand, you don't want your business to stop dead while you are out on a business call, shopping, or riding your bike, so an answering machine or message system is an essential communication support tool for any one- or two-person office.

If there is any single, modern anxiety heard from people halfway out their home office door, it's "Did I turn the answering machine on?" Buy a machine that you can turn on or off remotely by calling your number and letting it ring a certain number of times or punching a code. Also, look for a machine that can be set to pick up after three or four rings. This should give you plenty of time to grab the call live, and you can leave the machine on all the time. Most newer models interrupt the greeting tape the moment you pick up your receiver.

You will want an answering machine that you can call from anywhere to retrieve your messages and to leave new outgoing messages. Machines that allow incoming messages of any length are best, since cutting off callers after thirty or sixty seconds is a rude way to treat anyone. And avoid answering machines with preprogrammed, synthesized voices for outgoing greetings.

A good feature for some types of businesses is the "time stamp," which tells you exactly when a message came in. This helps you know how long someone has been waiting for you to return their call and helps you both if they neglect to say what time they are calling.

In many regions of the country, local phone companies offer computerized voice mail that improves on the answering-machine concept. These cost-effective services may eliminate the need for another piece of equipment taking space on your desk. And you won't need call waiting, because voice mail receives messages while you are talking to someone else. You can retrieve messages selectively, keep the ones you want, and erase the others. All in all, it sounds much more professional to callers than an answering machine.

Regardless of which type of answering system you select, have mercy on your callers. Avoid forcing them to listen to detailed instructions or your favorite musical selection. And humor is healthy, but not for outgoing messages. However droll your imitation of Robin Leach may be, it will sound unprofessional and will bore and annoy repeat callers. And avoid the common mistake, "We're not here right now," which is the invitation that burglars listen for.

Make your message brief and professional. "This is Mill Valley Carpentry. Please leave a message and we'll return your call shortly." If you have only one line for family and business calls, don't say, "You have reached the Swiss Tree Service and the Robinson residence. Leave a message for Bill, Robin, or Chris." Simply announce your business; your friends will know it's you. If you know someone with a good speaking voice, you may want to have them record the message for you, which is like having a secretary or assistant answer your own phone.

Fax Machines

The next time someone wonders aloud about what people did before the fax was invented, tell them, "They were fighting the Crimean War." The fax machine was around before the telephone and the typewriter. The Scottish electrician Alexander Bain invented the first facsimile machine in 1842. By 1853, a "copying telegraph" had been developed in England, and in 1924 the first wire photo was transmitted between two cities. Of course, these early transmissions were few and far between and their quality was poor by today's standards. Fax machines are now standard issue in just about every office, from log cabin home to skyscraper.

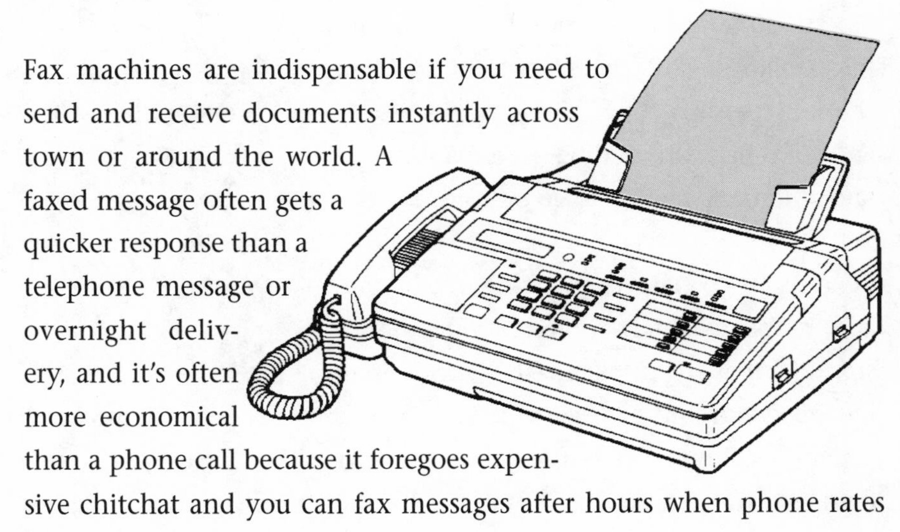

Fax machines are indispensable if you need to send and receive documents instantly across town or around the world. A faxed message often gets a quicker response than a telephone message or overnight delivery, and it's often more economical than a phone call because it foregoes expensive chitchat and you can fax messages after hours when phone rates are lower.

If you will be sending photos or detailed diagrams, be sure your fax machine has fine-resolution capability. Most non-plain-paper machines use 98-foot rolls of thermal paper, yielding about ninety standard-size sheets. This can be a handicap if you want your machine to receive lengthy documents unattended. In that case, you will want a machine that can hold 162-foot or 393-foot rolls. And unless you like to see a roll of paper snake its way through the room, choose a machine with an automatic paper cutter.

Baud refers to transmission speed. Some of the cheaper models run at 4,800 baud, but 9,600 baud is common and faster models are available. A faster fax can save you money if you will be faxing often and far. If you will be using your machine to transmit information to many different locations, look for a built-in autodialing feature.

A machine with a polling feature will automatically request faxes from other fax machines and is useful if you will be receiving reports from many locations. Some machines have polling security, which prevents an unauthorized person from calling your machine and automatically getting information contained in faxes waiting to go out.

Faxes to the Max

The Israeli national phone company, Bezek, recently opened a fax line to receive messages for God, which are sent by messenger to be stuffed into the crannies of the Wailing Wall in Jerusalem. The best prayers and messages are going to be published in a book. If you would like your prayer to be considered for publication, fax it to 972-2-235-555. If your prayer is confidential, the number is 972-2-612-222.

Be sure that whatever machine you choose accommodates the minimum and maximum size document you will need to send. Some machines have an oversize-document reduction feature. A ten-page or larger outgoing document feeder can save you lots of time when sending multipage documents. You don't want to be standing there feeding documents into a fax machine while your clothes go out of style.

If space in your office is tight, consider the size of the machine itself. You might be able to get away with a battery-powered portable fax small enough to fit into your briefcase. Some newer models stand vertically and occupy a relatively small footprint on your work surface.

You can save on phone-line installation and monthly fees by using one telephone line for both your phone and your fax. But a heavily used fax machine will need its own line and number. Some fax machines double as photocopiers, but if you plan on using it this way often, get a more expensive plain-paper model rather than one that uses thermal paper. Thermal copies don't survive well. If you receive an important document on thermal fax paper, make a photocopy right away.

Some models have an integrated phone, and a number of machines double as answering machines. But beware! If your integrated machine needs repair, you lose the answering machine while the system is in the repair depot.

If desk or room space is a serious concern, you can get an internal fax/modem for your computer. The fax receives transmissions by modem directly into your computer. You can then read the faxed material on screen or print it out on your printer. However, this arrangement doesn't let you transmit paper originals, like newspaper clippings and cartoons, to other fax machines, unless you have a scanner. And you have to leave your computer hooked up and turned on all the time—or in sleep mode, waiting to receive.

Copying Machines

If you choose a plain-paper fax machine, you have got a copier at your fingertips. If not, and you find yourself running to the copy shop more often than you would like, you may need your own personal copier.

I live in the country and am at the mercy of the copier at the general store, which charges twenty-five cents a page. Fortunately, I don't need to use it very often, and I make do with thermal copies on my fax machine in a pinch. But if the day comes when I add a real copying machine to my office, it will be the smallest one I can find.

When shopping around, beware of inexpensive copiers that will soak you when it's time to replace the toner cartridges. If you are making large quantities of copies, such as catalog sheets or newsletters, it might be more cost-effective to have them printed on an offset press or on an industrial-strength copier at a professional print or copy shop.

Resources

Consumer Reports magazine, published by the nonprofit Consumers Union, tests, reviews, and compares every imaginable consumer product—from computers, software, and other office equipment to insurance plans, airlines, automobiles, and toasters. It is available electronically through most major online services and is advertisement-free. A one-year subscription is under twenty-five dollars and includes the annual *Buying Guide.* Consumer Reports, Box 51166, Boulder, CO 80321-1166.

The "Hello Direct" catalog of telephone productivity tools includes short discussions and tips about setting up separate home-office lines and family lines, hands-free equipment, answering machines, auto-dialers, cellular phones, cords and connectors, and an array of other office electronic equipment. Hello Direct, 140 Great Oaks Boulevard, San Jose, CA 95119-9957. (800) 444-3556; fax, (408) 972-8155.

Mobile Office magazine is for laptop-computer users, cellular-phone aficionados, and business people on the move. Twelve monthly issues cost under twenty-five dollars. Mobile Office, P.O. Box 57267, Boulder, CO 80322-7267. (800) 627-5234.

15 Making Smart Software and Hardware Choices

During the past decade, many bright, energetic people got sidetracked by trying to understand the technology of personal computers. If the same thing had happened in the early days of the automobile, people would have sat around for years trying to learn how the carburetor worked, forgetting that the whole purpose of the automobile was to get them where they wanted to go. The most important thing you need to know about computers is how they can improve the quality of your life and make your world more productive and enjoyable.

Shopping for the Right Software

If you are anxious to buy your first computer or to replace your current one, hold on. Choose your software first. If you don't, you may find that the computer can't run the software you need, can't run it fast enough, or that the screen is too small and won't allow you to move around in the spreadsheet program or graphics package that is vital to your success.

First, narrow your focus to the few *types* of software that you will need. You can do this easily by listing your activities for a typical day or week. It might read like this:

Have lunch meeting with Jack to review spreadsheet & list of suppliers.

Outline speech for Independent Consultants Association convention. Review plastic recycling article in Omni magazine.

One-Stop Shopping

Some computers, such as the Apple Performa, come pre-loaded with application software for your particular business or profession. One version of the Performa, the Money Mac, has been loaded specifically for the home office and includes software for family financial management, a fax/modem, and a CD-ROM drive with a major encyclopedia. The beauty of buying such a turnkey system is that all the hardware and software decisions have been made for you and you know everything is going to work when you plug it in.

This little scenario would make good use of spreadsheet and word-processing software and a telecommunications package to get the text of the *Omni* article from an electronic database service.

Use the following list to check off the things you need to do in each application category.

If any of your activities aren't on the checklist, add them. Bring the checklist to a friend or business associate who uses current versions of these types of software and ask for a demonstration. Or find a computer store that is patient with customers, reputable, and support-minded. Bear in mind that these demos are to help you get the feel of various kinds of software and to compare competing word-processing software packages and other applications. Your friend's favorite desktop-publishing program could be overpowered or overpriced for your needs.

Try to read through the instruction manual before you buy any product. Be sure it includes a "quick start" section and a tutorial. It should explain things clearly, in plain language, and it should be well organized and indexed. If it isn't, you will lose a lot of the time you gain from being computerized to manual labor.

Checklist of Software Applications

Word Processing

- ❐ Articles
- ❐ Books
- ❐ Brochures
- ❐ Letters
- ❐ Memos
- ❐ Newsletters
- ❐ Press releases
- ❐ Reports
- ❐ Other ________________

Databases

- ❐ Phone lists
- ❐ Mailing lists
- ❐ Product and parts lists
- ❐ Stock inventory
- ❐ Subscription and mail-order fulfillment
- ❐ Supplier lists
- ❐ Client or customer lists
- ❐ Other ________________

Desktop Publishing

- ❐ Designing publications
- ❐ Photographic enhancement and manipulation
- ❐ Other ________________

Graphics

- ❐ Charts
- ❐ Graphs
- ❐ Tables
- ❐ Text
- ❐ Photography
- ❐ Designing labels and trademarks
- ❐ Architectural rendering
- ❐ Industrial design
- ❐ Other ________________

Multimedia

- ❐ Animation and storyboards
- ❐ Music composition
- ❐ Interactive books, games, and other applications
- ❐ Other ________________

Money Management and Statistical Packages

- ❐ Tax preparation
- ❐ Accounting, check writing, bookkeeping, invoicing, receivables
- ❐ Financial analysis
- ❐ Forecasts
- ❐ Budgets
- ❐ Complex equations and formulas
- ❐ Other ________________

Spreadsheets

- ❐ Cash flow
- ❐ Inventory
- ❐ Producing profit and loss statements
- ❐ Producing balance sheets
- ❐ Tracking project schedules and costs
- ❐ What-if modeling
- ❐ Other ________________

(Continued on Next Page)

Checklist of Software Applications *(Continued)*

Telecommunications

- ❒ E-mail (electronic mail)
- ❒ Faxing
- ❒ Information acquisition
- ❒ Business news
- ❒ Daily local and world news
- ❒ Economic reports
- ❒ Reference and research
- ❒ Lodging, dining, and other reservations
- ❒ Stock quotes
- ❒ Shopping for goods and services
- ❒ Transportation schedules
- ❒ Other ________________

Find out how software upgrades are handled. New versions are inevitable and should be available for a discount to registered owners of the previous version. *Test drive it,* if possible, or get a thirty-day guarantee of satisfaction.

You can often save money by buying software through a mail-order catalog. However, buying it from a reputable dealer who will give you support if you need it may be worth every penny of the retail price. (The exception is for experienced buyers who know what they want and are willing to get their support by telephone.)

You can also get free or almost-free software by downloading it from the various online information utilities, such as CompuServe and America Online. Be careful, though, as there is always a chance of computer viruses accompanying software from unknown sources. The most common way to infect your computer system is to let other people run *their* disks on your computer. If you expect to share your machine, you should buy and install anti-viral software.

Computer user groups are an excellent resource for beginners. They can provide support if computer and software problems arise and offer suggestions to enhance your skills. They are great sources for "shareware," software shared free or for a small license fee. User groups help make computing an ongoing social and educational experience. They are not only good forums for meeting others with similar equipment, but are communities where friendly people share your business, professional, and academic interests. Computer dealers can provide a list of computer user groups, and you will see ads for them in the classified sections of free computer publications distributed in sidewalk boxes, bookstores, cafes, and computer stores across the country. Their meetings are often listed in the calendar of your local newspaper.

Shopping for the Right Hardware

The software you decide to buy will determine, to a large extent, how much computer you need. A computer is an organizing tool. Aim a computer at words and paragraphs, and it's a word processor. Aim one at graphic design and text problems, and it's a desktop-publishing system. Aim one at figures, and it's a number-cruncher that accomplishes in seconds what once took hours or days. You don't have to know much about how a computer works to take advantage of its power. But you do need to know a few basics to make an intelligent purchase.

An integrated package—such as Microsoft Works for IBM and compatible computers and Claris Works for Macintosh computers—incorporates a variety of capabilities in one software package. The various functions—managing your contacts, calendars, to-do lists, appointments, alarms, personal information, letter writing, and telecommunications—interact, so you can plug figures from a spreadsheet into a letter and perform other data-sharing activities.

RAM (Random Access Memory) is the memory the computer uses to keep things running. It also keeps your work, such as a letter you are writing, alive until you store it on your disk. It's comparable to the size of your desk area: the bigger it is, the more things you can work on at once.

The amount of RAM you will need is determined by the software you will be running. Word processors tend to require the least amount of RAM, while graphics and multimedia software require the most. RAM comes on built-in chips, and you can easily get additional RAM chips plugged into your computer if it has extra chip slots available. A rule of thumb is that 4 megabytes (MB) of RAM will probably serve the non-power user adequately. But the more RAM you have, the more easily you can add increasingly powerful software to allow you to perform tasks and move between actions ever more quickly. And more RAM will allow you to keep a number of applications open and active simultaneously without running out of memory.

If later on you decide you need more RAM, there are software packages available that will allow you to effectively increase your RAM without buying more hardware. Check with your knowledgeable friends or local computer dealers.

RAM is "volatile" memory, meaning that it shuts down when you turn

Around the World in Twenty Minutes

"If the aircraft industry had evolved as spectacularly as the computer industry over the past 25 years, a Boeing 767 would cost $500 today and it would circumnavigate the globe in 20 minutes on five gallons of fuel. Such performance would represent a rough analog of the reduction in cost, the increase in speed of operation and the decrease in energy consumption of computers."

From the March 1983 *Scientific American – more than a decade ago!*

off the computer. Hard disk memory, on the other hand, remains in your computer all the time. The hard disk is like an electronic file cabinet: the larger it is, the more information you can store. But like your file cabinet, sooner or later you will fill it up. Probably sooner. Start with at least a 40-MB hard drive, which can store approximately forty times the amount of text in this book. If you can afford a bigger one, you might as well get it now.

You may also want to consider purchasing a CD-ROM drive. CD-ROM is based on the same technology that packs a lot of music onto a compact disk or into a high-resolution movie for playback on your TV set. CD-ROM disks have sound and interactive capabilities and store mountains of information, such as complete illustrated encyclopedias. They are especially good for reference material, photographs, music, and other prepackaged data, but the technology is not yet practical for storing your own creations.

Many other storage devices are available. As with software, your best source of information and advice will be friends or colleagues in your field.

The cost of getting set up properly varies according to the tasks to be done. A writer really needs little more than a personal computer with 4 MB of RAM, a 40-MB hard disk, and a simple printer. Graphic designers and multimedia mavens need a much larger hard disk, a large color monitor, and a lot more RAM to manipulate images and sound.

Regardless of what computer you choose, a zippier model is always about to be released, and yours will be virtually obsolete the moment you plug it in. The point is to invest now in a machine that will serve your needs far into the future. Choose carefully, overbuy if you can afford to, and enjoy what you get for a number years to come. Most computers can be upgraded later.

Don't worry if you are feeling bewildered. You can always hire a computer consultant to help you determine your software and hardware needs and specify what you should buy. You can find a consultant by personal referral, through a local computer user group, or in the classified section of your local computer newspaper or magazine. You can also find expert advice, plus software and hardware reviews, in major computer magazines such as *Home Office Computing, PC World, MacWorld, and MacHome Companion.*

Once you have selected your computer equipment, consider getting a backup emergency power supply that will kick in automatically if your house current is suddenly reduced or shut off. Rural electrical systems go down because of wet weather, and urban centers suffer outages when there's a huge demand on the system by air conditioners or heaters. If you are writing the great American novel and a squirrel bites through a power line near your home, a battery backup will give you time to save what you are working on and perhaps let you continue entering those

Plugging In

If your computer was manufactured before 1993, don't leave it on overnight because the bill for the electricity it uses idling can really add up. Newer computers are being built to new government standards and are much easier on the environment. They have microprocessors that operate at lower voltages and sleep modes that kick in after the machine has been idling for a while. The Environmental Protection Agency estimates that these newer computers will save twenty-six billion kilowatt hours of electricity annually nationwide, enough to power New Hampshire, Vermont, and Maine for a year.

If you get a laser printer, don't leave it on all day unless you are using it all day. Turning your printer on and off won't wear it out and is kinder on the environment. If you can, wait to print everything at once, or do a print session in the morning and another in the afternoon to save electricity and money.

inspired phrases while other novelists in the neighborhood must quit. Whether or not you invest in a battery backup, you should get a surge suppresser to protect your equipment from electrical spikes that can occur when the power is restored and that can fry computers and other electronic goodies. They are inexpensive and simply plug into your electrical outlet.

Laptop Computers

Marvelous as they are, desktop computers force you to do your computing at the desk where they live. Today's powerful laptop computers can go wherever you go. The burden of having to sit at the same desk, at the same address, staring at the one-eyed monster can be a thing of the past.

I unchained myself back in 1982 when the TRS-80 Model 100 was introduced. I paid thirteen hundred dollars for that three-pound beauty that sported a mere 32K of RAM. I took it to the top of Haleakala volcano on Maui, where I wrote a chapter about portable computing. Without a disk drive, all the machine could handle was about thirty-two pages of text. But that's all I needed. When I came down from the crater, I plugged the computer into a telephone jack and sent the chapter to my publisher in New York. It was exhilarating.

A decade later I bought my Apple PowerBook laptop for a similar amount of money. But it came with 4MB of RAM and a 40-MB hard drive. I used it to write this book—in bed, at the beach, on airplanes, and out on my deck. And I often use it in my office.

Most laptop computers let you do everything a desktop model does. They are available with black-and-white or color screens, and because their screens aren't cathode-ray tubes, you may experience less eye strain than with your standard computer even after many hours of use. If the screen is too small for some of your uses, such as page layout and graphic design projects, many models can be connected to a large external monitor. When equipped with an internal or external modem, a laptop lets you tap into powerful information utilities anywhere there's a phone jack. There are even some wireless models that communicate over the cellular telephone network.

The First "Word Processor"

In 1894 Mark Twain plunked down $125—a bundle in those days—for a Remington Model I typewriter. He was one of the first authors to buy this piece of equipment. Twain later wrote, "The machine has several virtues.... One may lean back in his chair and work it. It piles an awful stack of words on one page. It don't muss things or scatter ink blots around."

The major downside to laptops is that they run on a rechargeable battery, many of which last only two to four hours before you must insert a freshly charged battery or plug the computer into an AC outlet. But that's a minor inconvenience compared to how empowering and liberating it is to carry around your knowledge base. Buy the smallest, lightest, most powerful machine that frees your imagination and your body. Now that's living!

If you still feel trepidation at the prospect of buying and using a computer but need some kind of organizational support, consider starting with a small personal organizer, such as the Sharp Wizard or the Casio

Boss. They will fit in your pocket or purse and will store phone numbers, addresses, and important dates, and help you manage your schedule. Some advanced models, with optional accessories, can share data with computers, send faxes, and access online database services. They provide a good way for technophobes to warm up to computing and are an inexpensive way to get some leverage on your information-management needs. Most accept short notes, and some can hook up to computer printers.

Printers

Once you have your computer, you will need a printer so your work won't just hover in the ether of virtual greatness, but can be turned into hard copy. There are three basic types of printers from which to choose:

- Dot-matrix printers, what computers grew up with, give a very fast but mechanical-looking printout. This impact-type printer is essential if you want to print multipart NCR (no carbon required) forms.
- Ink-jet printers are compact and make a perfect companion for a laptop computer.
- A laser printer, more expensive than the other two types, is a must if you will be printing letters, brochures, or other materials that must look professional.

Once your home office is computerized to the level that serves your needs, don't forget the pleasures of that old-fashioned, low-tech standby, the fountain pen. Send occasional handwritten notes and letters. Your recipients will appreciate the human touch in a world where the overwhelming majority of paper and electronic communication has a mechanical appearance without much character. It was noted more than a decade ago that as we embrace "high tech" we will increasingly seek "high touch."

16 *The Magic of Going Online*

People who never thought a computer would be of much use to them are now discovering that a computerized information utility can shorten the time required to locate information from days to minutes. I, for example, now live so far from a well-stocked public library that electronic research has become indispensable. I can call up an online communications service, search for magazine articles by key words, download them to my computer, and print them out.

If you connect to Internet, or to one of the major information utilities, you will have nearly instant access to hundreds of databases: from airline schedules to condominiums for rent; from special-interest groups on every subject to fairs and festivals; from movie reviews to free software. You can read breaking news stories or review old news stories selected by subject, region, date, company name, or the name of anyone or any thing mentioned in them.

Information utilities also provide global networking through electronic mail. E-mail consists of text and graphics sent and received between computers via modem and phone lines, with an intermediary service that routes the mail to the right mailboxes. I have been using E-mail for over a decade to communicate with editors and with clients and correspondents in other countries. You can use it to receive and send letters and faxes to people around the world.

You can also get access to electronic bulletin board services, or BBS's, a sort of "classified section" for people with common interests who wish to buy, sell, trade, or just chat about an amazing range of subjects. You can describe yourself and your business, and people from all over will exchange information, jokes, and personal thoughts with you. You can communicate about topics of mutual interest with strangers who may easily become friends and colleagues. Some BBS's require a subscription fee, but many are free. You can also use telecommunications for Telex and TWX messaging, electronic banking, shopping, and ticketing and reservation services.

To take advantage of all this power, you will need a modem and telecommunications software. Modems connect your computer to a phone line through which you access online services. You can purchase an external modem or have one installed in your computer. They operate at varying speeds—the faster ones cost more, but if you will be using online services often, you will make it up on your phone bill. When it comes to telecommunications, time really *is* money!

Here is a brief look at a few of the major online telecommunications services. For additional information on rates and services, give them a call.

MCI Mail was established a decade ago and was the first E-mail service to provide accessible rates for individuals and small businesses. I subscribed to MCI Mail in 1983 and sent text I created on my first laptop from remote places in the U.S. and abroad to my own MCI mailbox. When I returned home, I used my Macintosh computer to call myself up, download the files, and continue my work. I also use this service to exchange short letters and draft chapters of books with friends and editors. MCI also lets you cost-effectively send E-mail to people on other electronic networks. The annual membership fee is about thirty-five dollars, which gives you access to a toll-free connect line. You are billed by the amount of data you send. MCI, (800) 444-6245.

America Online offers a world of information, software reviews, free software, technical support, personal communication, multiplayer games, mail-order shopping, homework help, an entrée into a wide array of interest groups, and interactive classes for children and adults. It's very popular and has an easy interface for navigating around the service. The cost is about ten dollars per month for five hours, with an additional charge for each extra hour. You can even get a free test drive. America Online, (800) 827-6364.

CompuServe provides E-mail and online magazines such as *Consumer Reports*. You can purchase goods from such retailers as Land's End and JC Penney and get news from Associated Press and stock reports from Quick & Reilly. CompuServe prides itself on having members from all walks of life, from shepherds to rocket scientists. Mensa, the high IQ society, uses it for their online meetings. CompuServe provides a forum for active debate about social issues. Of course, you can find these things on most networks, but CompuServe is a community with an enthusiastic spirit of camaraderie. I use this service to exchange letters and other text with correspondents in the U.S., Europe, and Asia. I compose off-line, then send a letter in one or two minutes that would take much longer to say at international phone rates. E-mail doesn't replace personal calls, of course, but it does supplement communications and is instantaneous—unlike the world's postal services. The Extended Electronic Communications service lets you send mail to MCI Mail, Telex, Internet, AT&T 400, Western Union 400, and fax addresses anywhere in the world. There's also a "CB simulator" for real-time (live) conversations, and you don't have to be a member of Mensa to use the easy interface, Information Manager, to surf around in cyberspace. The cost of about nine dollars per month includes unlimited use of seventy services. CompuServe, (800) 848-8199.

GEnie provides more than one hundred products and services, including multiplayer games; trademark registration; and interest-group bulletin boards where you can leave questions, post messages, and share ideas on subjects ranging from religion to real estate. Every bulletin board subject has a RoundTable, which has software libraries and allows real-time conferences. GEnie gives you news, weather, and sports; airline, hotel, and rental car bookings; stock and mutual fund closings—you name it. You can access Grolier's Electronic Encyclopedia, a ten-million word database that is updated quarterly. There's a vast library of shareware you can download for a small fee or for free, "chatlines" with celebrities like Michael Crichton, and conferences you can participate in with experts. A money-back guarantee makes it even better. The cost is about nine dollars per month for four hours, with an additional fee for each extra hour. Call GEnie at (800) 638-9636

Prodigy is well-suited for the whole family and has more than two million subscribers. As with other online services, you can shop, bank electronically, check news and worldwide weather, access an encyclopedia, and communicate with people from every interest group imaginable. Prodigy recently linked up with Sierra Network, the nationwide "electronic amusement park" famous for its real-time, multiplayer, interactive games. Subscribers in different parts of the country can play against each other while chatting through their keyboards. The cost is about fifteen dollars per month. Prodigy, (800) 776-3449.

Internet was born out of Pentagon research years ago and now serves the public by linking up electronic services worldwide. Until recently, sending E-mail or other data from one computer network to another required a lot of phone calls, complicated parameter-matching, and a great deal of luck. But the Internet allows information—including live video—to move easily from one network to another. Although it's still in the formative stage, Internet's success is reflected in astounding numbers: As of September 1993, approximately seventeen million users were connected in 137 countries. It carries the world's largest electronic bulletin board, with over thirty-five hundred topics. Internet can be reached at (800) 646-3869. For easy access to Internet, you can subscribe to Delphi, another leading service, which offers a five-hour free Internet trial in evenings and on weekends. After your free trial you can choose from two low-cost Delphi membership plans, with rates as low as one dollar per hour. To start your free trial, dial (800) 365-4636 by modem, press return once or twice, and at *Password* enter SFC12321. If you have questions, call (800) 695-4005 to speak to someone at Delphi.

There are other ways into Internet. For example, Prodigy's Mail Manger puts you in touch with Internet mail and other online services, and Microsoft Windows' forthcoming Version 4.0 will include built-in Internet access, allowing people to "plug" directly into Internet without any complex setups. Many educational institutions have Internet accounts and allow people with institutional connections, such as students and lecturers, to use them. This can be important, since full access to Internet may be an expensive prospect for an individual user.

The WELL was founded by editors and writers at *Whole Earth Review* and serves some of the most advanced thinkers in the world. It's an exciting forum and the place to go for conferences and bulletin boards about ecology, alternative lifestyles, architecture, cybernetics, and other leading-edge interests. The WELL, (415) 332-4335.

17 Protecting Your Health and Home

You will gain immeasurable benefits by heading out on your own. However, you are also going to give up a little—most noticeably the benefits that have been attached to your salary.

One of the most important benefits you must provide for yourself is health-care coverage. Even on your own, you can buy quality coverage at group rates by joining one of the many local and national associations of home-based businesses. In addition to group medical insurance, these associations provide members with lots of valuable information.

One such organization, the National Association for the Self-Employed, founded in 1981, has 320,000 members nationwide. It publishes *Self-Employed America* six times a year, which covers financial and business issues including legislation, time management, venture capital, and marketing and trade shows. In addition to health-care coverage, NASE members qualify for discounts on overnight shipping, travel arrangements, and a sophisticated range of long-distance phone services. NASE has advocates who work with state and federal legislators and maintains an 800 number for access to its small-business consultants. National Association for the Self-Employed, 2121 Precinct Line Road, Hurst, TX 76054. (800) 232-6273.

In addition to health insurance, your coverage should include income replacement in case of disability. Being put out of action even temporarily because of accident or illness could destroy everything you have built. Disability insurance is so expensive, however, that many small-business owners self-insure. That is, they maintain a savings account for the sole purpose of paying the bills for at least three months in the event that they are unable to work. Such savings, however, would still be dreadfully inadequate in the case of a catastrophic accident or illness.

You will also need business insurance, since your homeowner's or renter's policy may not cover accidents that occur in your home as a result of doing business from your residence. Discuss covering your business for injury liability with your insurance agent, especially if you will have clients visiting your home office—in case someone trips on the pink plastic flamingo stuck in your lawn!

If you don't purchase business insurance, your homeowner's or renter's policy should be supported with an itemized inventory of your valuables, including photographs or videotapes of furniture, art objects, antiques, and other equipment. With this documentation you can support your claim in case of fire, burglary, earthquake, or other catastrophe. Photograph large items in their usual position in your home; group smaller items together and photograph them on a neutral background. Keep copies of the pictures or negatives in a home safe, or better yet, in a bank safe-deposit box. And don't forget to photograph and list additional items as you acquire them.

It may also be wise to obtain professional liability coverage, which is similar to medical or legal malpractice insurance. It covers you in the event a client thinks you have failed to live up to contractual terms and that the client has been damaged as a result, and it may also pay your legal fees in addition to damages if you are found liable. We are a litigious nation, and independent businesses and professionals must protect themselves just as corporations do. In the end, it might be best to buy an umbrella policy that insures you against everything imaginable except your own gross or willful negligence.

Since you will be spending more time at home than regular workers, and at unpredictable hours, you are somewhat less likely to be the target of a burglar. But there will be little joy working from home if you lose anything to a heist. To reduce the chance that a burglar will zero in on your home office, don't list your physical address in the telephone book. And your answering machine's outgoing message shouldn't say, "I'm not here right now," which translates as, "Come help yourself to my office equipment." Instead, you might say you are unable to come to the phone or are on another line.

The last thing a burglar wants to encounter, however, is the sound of a loudly barking dog.

When you do go out, leave a radio or TV on to give a would-be intruder the impression someone is inside. To keep the place looking lived in at night, plug two or three lights into timers and set them to turn off around your normal bedtime. You can leave a bathroom light on all night long, since anyone watching your house might expect that room to be in use any time. A motion-detecting light outside can be useful, but they can be triggered by cats and deer as well as prowlers.

If you are very concerned about burglary, you might want to invest in a sophisticated security system. Some now available at reasonable cost will not only trigger an on-site alarm, but will also signal you on your pager when you are away.

Ultimately, you are the one who can best protect your most valuable asset: data and knowledge, most of which may be on your computer disks. Computer users often learn the hard way that they must make backups of important work, records, and programs, and store them away from the office. Can you imagine anyone writing in the days of typewriters and pens not making carbon copies? In case of a computer crash, burglary, fire, or coffee spill, you will come to a sad end with no backups. Making backups is common sense and vital insurance.

18 An Invitation From the Author

The renowned mythologist Joseph Campbell was once challenged to come up with a nugget of wisdom common among all the world's cultures. He responded without hesitation, "Follow your bliss!"

Some years ago I met Bill Helbing, who teaches philosophy at the University of Hawaii. Bill subscribes to the Buddhist way of "right livelihood"—doing what he loves to do and what is natural to him. The money comes as a result of "right actions," not from chasing money for its own sake. Fifteen years ago Bill became alarmed at the rapid disappearance of much of Hawaii's native flora, and began cultivating some of the most endangered plants at his home on the Big Island of Hawaii. He now sells them to his neighbors and to commercial nurseries on the island. As the head of a family with four children, he makes good use of the extra income.

Bill is following his bliss. This isn't work; it's something he does for pleasure. It helps bring him and his family close to nature while serving the community at the same time. And he does it with an absolute minimum of technology: a shovel, a rake, a telephone, and a small truck.

Bill has thirty mountain acres in Hawaii for his enterprise. But much can be grown, assembled, drawn, and otherwise cooked up in a small space on an apartment balcony, in a rural cottage, or on a suburban estate. The space required most is that of spirit and imagination. You have a right to work as you will—and to thrive.

Towards the end of writing this book I discovered *The Romance of Business,* written in 1917 by Elbert Hubbard, while browsing in a rural antique store. Hubbard, one of that era's leading humanists, founded the Roycrofters in upstate New York, a guild of printers, furniture makers, and coppersmiths who lived on a large, profitable, cooperative estate. "Commerce is no longer exploitation," Hubbard wrote. "It is human service, and no business concern can hope to prosper which does not meet a human need and add to human happiness. We are moving toward the sunrising, and no man can guess the splendor and the riches and the beauty that will yet be ours. Let America lead the way!"

With the current growth of independent, home-based businesses, Hubbard's sentiment rings especially true today. Enterprise is the workshop where we care for our customers, our families, and the common good. Small business is not just a way to make money, but a way to add meaning to our community life.

I hope that, in reading this book, you have gained insight into your own potential and the possibility of balancing your life and your living. You've read about others who have made a life working independently, and you have heard some of my stories. Now I invite you to share *your* story with me. Let me know how you're doing. Write to me at P.O. Box 244, Dillon Beach, CA 94929. My America Online name is simply, "JeffBerner." Good luck, and stay in touch.

Jeff Berner

The Home Office Tax Deduction

Although writing checks to the IRS may not qualify as one of the joys of working from home, it is a pleasure to know that your home office can earn you substantial tax advantages. If you are just starting a business, however, you may find you don't have enough income to make the deduction worth the trouble. That's because home office expenses (other than mortgage interest and real estate taxes, which are deductible in full anyway) cannot be used to create a business loss. For example, if you have a one-hundred-dollar profit, you can only take a one-hundred-dollar home office deduction. But if you are making tons of money, the home office deduction can be quite advantageous.

Home Office Deduction Requirements

You can take a limited deduction for your home if you use it *exclusively* and *regularly:*

- As the principal place of business for any trade or business you are in
- As a place to meet or deal with patients, clients, or customers in the normal course of your trade or business
- In connection with your trade or business if you are using a separate structure unattached to your house or residence, such as a garage where you store inventory

To deduct the use of part of your home as a business, you must use that part of your home *exclusively and regularly* as your principal place of business, or as a place to meet or deal with patients, customers, or clients in the normal course of business. If you are a consultant who meets with clients and has no other place of business, you will breeze right through this requirement. But the IRS gets much stickier with people who work elsewhere, such as doctors who practice at hospitals but do their billing and paperwork at home.

If you are an employee, you won't be able to take any deduction for the business use of your home even if you meet the exclusive and regular use tests. However, you may still be allowed to take deductions for the furniture and equipment you use for your business or work. Telecommuters should pay particular attention to this part of the law and consult a tax advisor, as individual facts and circumstances make a big difference.

Tips on Taking Home Office Deductions

- Make sure your office is a separate, distinct space used only for business.
- Keep good records right from the start to show that your business really is a business.
- Include an explanation with your return of how your office is used so the IRS will have a clear picture of what you are basing your deduction claims on. Send a photo if necessary.
- Exclude the value of land when setting the value of your home to calculate the depreciation for the portion used as a home office.
- Remember that home office expenses can't be used to create a business loss, but unused expenses can be carried forward.

If you are going to claim a home office deduction, you will have to file Form 8829, Expenses for Business Use of Your Home. To avoid being red-flagged for an audit, attach an explanation or even a photo of your work area so the IRS agent can see how your office is used. This strategy is recommended by Harvey A. Brown, a tax attorney and professor of business at Cuyahoga Community College in Cleveland. In twenty-five years, he has never had a client's home office deduction questioned.

If you take the home office deduction, keep a detailed log of what you did and with whom you met or had lunch with, including brief notes about the business agenda. If you are self-employed, keeping separate phone and bank accounts and using proper expense vouchers will go a long way toward demonstrating to the IRS that your home office is legitimate.

Keep every receipt and canceled check that applies to you personally and professionally in a safe place for at least five years. The IRS may look at your car, home, and wing-tipped shoes and estimate how much you are making. Whether or not their estimate of your income and any additional tax claim is correct, you will have no legal defense if you don't have good, organized records of income and expenses. A shoe box full of receipts, canceled checks, and income vouchers is a start, but if you show up for an audit with the box you may flunk the "attitude test." Keeping organized records can make an audit an essentially pleasant, educational experience.

The Language of Deductions

Before you get too excited about home office deductions, you should know how the IRS defines certain terms.

Trade or Business Use. You must use your home in connection with a trade or business to take a deduction for its business use. If you use your home for a profit-seeking activity that only requires reading financial periodicals and reports or clipping bond coupons for your own investments, you cannot take the deduction.

Exclusive Use. You must use the part of your home for which you want to claim a deduction for business only. If you are an attorney and you use your den to write legal briefs and prepare client tax returns but also to watch television, you cannot claim a business deduction for it. There are two exceptions: You can still claim a deduction if you use part of your home, such as your garage, to store inventory; or if you use part of your home, such as the family room, as a day-care facility.

Storage of Inventory. You can deduct expenses for the storage of inventory in part of your home if you meet all of the following tests:

- The inventory is for use in your trade or business.
- Your trade or business is the wholesale or retail selling of products.
- Your home is the only fixed location of your trade or business.
- You use the storage space on a regular basis.
- The space you use is a separate, identifiable space that is suitable for storage.

For example, if you sell mechanics' tools at retail and you regularly use half your basement to store inventory and the other half for personal purposes (such as throwing parties), expenses for the storage space—such as custom-built shelving or lockers—*are* deductible.

Regular Use. Occasional or incidental business use of part of your home does not meet the regular use test, even if that part is used for no other purpose.

Principal Place of Business. Whether your home is considered the principal place of business for your trade or business depends on the total time you spend working there, its facilities, and the relative amount of income you get from working there.

You can have a principal place of business for each trade or business in which you engage. For example, a teacher's principal place of business for teaching is a school. If the teacher also engages in retail selling and uses a part of the home as the principal place for this business, expenses for this business use of the home may be deductible.

Even if you have more than one location for a single trade or business, you can still deduct expenses for your home office if your home is your principal place of business. Ted Brannagan is an outside salesperson for a large company. His only office is a room in his home that he uses only for business and where he spends a substantial amount of time maintaining business records and making appointments. Therefore, his home qualifies as his principle place of business.

Place to Meet Patients, Clients, or Customers. If you meet or deal with patients, clients, or customers in your home in the normal course of your business—even though you also carry on business at another location—you can deduct your expenses for the part of your home used exclusively and regularly for business. This applies only to the part of your home visited by your clients. It doesn't apply to a room where you make or receive phone calls but don't meet with clients. Ophelia Merrymount, a chiropractor, works three days a week in her city office and two days a week in her home office, where she treats clients. Her home office qualifies for a business deduction because she meets clients there in the normal course of her business.

You can also deduct expenses for a separate freestanding structure, such as a studio, garage, barn, or greenhouse, if you use the structure exclusively and regularly for your business. The structure does not have to be your principal place of business or a place where you meet patients, clients, or customers. Christina Alvarado operates a floral shop in town and grows the plants for her shop in a greenhouse behind her home. Since she uses the greenhouse exclusively and regularly in her business, she can deduct the expenses for its use.

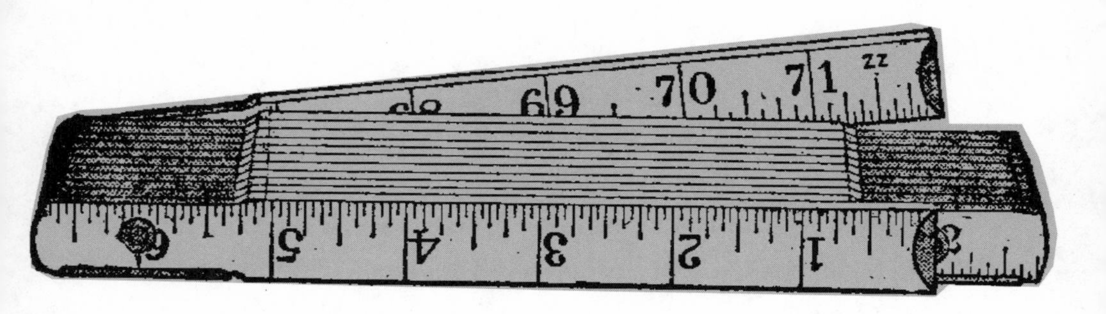

Figuring the Business Percentages

The amount you are entitled to deduct is based on the square footage of your workspace as a percentage of the total floor space in your home. You must first determine what percentage of your home is used for business by dividing the square footage used for business by the total square footage in your home. For example, if your home measures 1,200 square feet and you use one room that measures 240 square feet for business, you would divide 240 by 1,200. Multiply the answer by 100 to get the percentage of the total area used for business; in this case, 20 percent.

If the rooms in your home are about the same size, you can divide the number of rooms used for your business by the total number of rooms in the home. For example, if you use one room in a five-room home for business, divide 1 by 5 and then multiply by 100 to get 20 percent.

Expenses for utilities and services, such as electricity, gas, trash removal, and for cleaning services are also deductible when you use part of your home for business. Best of all, you don't have to qualify for the home office deduction to deduct these expenses. The calculations, also based on the business percentage, can be a little tricky. For example, your electric bill includes electricity used for lighting, cooking, laundry, and television. But only the lighting is used for business, so you must determine what portion of your bill is for lighting alone, then multiply that amount by the business percentage. For example, if you determine that

$250 of your electric bill is for lighting and you use 10 percent of your home for business, $25 is deductible as a business expense.

The basic local telephone service charge, including taxes, for the first telephone line into your home is not deductible. However, charges for long-distance business calls on that line—and the cost of a second line into your home used exclusively for business—are. If you are self-employed, these expenses are not deducted on form 8829 but are included on Schedule C, Profit or Loss from Business.

The rules applying to home office deductions are very specific. Come filing time, you and your tax advisor may look at the numbers and new rules and decide not to take a home office deduction. That doesn't mean your efforts have been wasted, as you will have established a system for figuring home office deductions in the future when you might need it. And, if you are self-employed, you will already have some of the documentation you will need to deduct some business expenses on your Schedule C.

Resources

The most reliable source of information on the home office deduction is the IRS. Publication 530, Tax Information for First-Time Homeowners; Publication 936, Home Mortgage Interest Deduction; and Publication 587, Business Use of Your Home, are available free at local IRS offices or by calling (800) 829-3676. (Good luck getting through!)

APPENDIX B *Self-Employment and the IRS*

If you have been working on a salaried basis, your taxes and benefit contributions were deducted from your salary automatically. What you took home you got to keep. Once you become self-employed, you will want to change your frame of mind. If you make a sale or sign a contract for five thousand dollars, you might think you have just "made" that much money. In reality, you will be liable for a certain percentage of it at tax time.

A large percentage of home-based workers fall under the category of independent contractors. An individual doing bookkeeping and related services for several clients is an independent contractor, and income from this work is considered self-employment income. If, however, you perform the same services under the control of an employer who tells you what will be done and how it will be done, an employer-employee relationships exists and you are not considered self-employed.

Schedule C

Income from self-employment—including work you do on the side in addition to your regular job—is reported on Schedule C. If your business has gross receipts of $25,000 or less and you are claiming no more than $2,000 in business expenses, you can use Schedule C-EZ. Like 1040EZ, this form is short and sweet and asks only eight questions instead of the forty questions on Schedule C. To determine your estimated tax, simply look up the amount you owe on the expanded tax tables, which provide the precalculated tax for earnings of $100,000 or less. If you are bringing in more than that, you probably won't be doing your own taxes!

Tax-preparation software packages, available for both IBM and Macintosh computers, incorporate the federal tax code for the specific tax year, and some provide state income tax requirements. Some twelve million taxpayers are currently using such software to do their taxes relatively painlessly. Many tax-preparation software packages are integrated with easy-to-use money management and check-writing programs. They can tell you your tax liability throughout the year, helping you anticipate your taxes as your income ebbs and flows. If you have a computer, I highly recommend you look into one of these packages.

Regardless of how you prepare your taxes, remember that tax law has many tricky areas, such as depreciation, and the rules may have changed by the time the ink dries on these pages. If possible, enlist the services of a qualified expert, particularly if you are just starting out.

Self-Employment Tax

In addition to income tax, you must pay self-employment tax if you have net earnings from self-employment of four hundred dollars or more. This is a 15-percent Social Security and Medicare tax for people who work for themselves. If you were previously employed, your employer paid half of this tax. Once you are on your own, you are responsible for the full amount. The tax due on net earnings from self-employment is reported on Schedule SE. For an explanation of the benefits available to you and your family under the Social Security program, or to get a Social Security number or card if you don't already have one, consult your nearest Social Security office.

Partnerships

If you and your spouse operate a business together and share in the profits and losses, you have a partnership and must report the business income on Form 1065. You will each also need to fill out Schedule K-1 to show each partner's share of the net income and file separate Schedule SE's to report the self-employment tax. If your spouse is not your partner but your employee, you must pay Social Security and Medicare taxes for him or her. IRS Publication 937 has further details.

There's a lot more to know about the tax benefits and liabilities of self-employment. The various IRS publications will provide you with current information on specific points of tax law, but if this kind of figuring isn't your cup of tea, enlist the help of a tax consultant who specializes in self-employment.

Resources

The IRS publishes several handy references, including Publication 334, Tax Guide for Small Business; Publication 533, Self-Employment Tax; and Publication 910, Free Tax Services. They are all available free at your local IRS office or by calling (800) 829-3676. You can also get live telephone tax assistance by calling (800) 829-1040. Tax assistance for the hearing impaired who have access to TDD equipment is available at (800) 829-4059.

APPENDIX

Further Resources to Help You Succeed

These resources will help you further explore the issues associated with working from home.

Books

Homemade Money, by Barbara Brabec, is a compendium of home-based business advice and lore that has been published and revised since 1984. The current edition is 325 pages long and has advice for almost every type of business, from cottage industries to consulting professions. The book is available for $21.95 from the author at P.O. Box 2137, Naperville, IL 60567.

The Entrepreneur's Bookshelf, edited by Edie Levenson, is a "book of books" that briefly describes and annotates books for the entrepreneur. It lists books on choosing the right business; networking; negotiating; finance and accounting; and marketing, advertising, and publicity. It includes author credentials and ordering information for each title. Contact Edie Levenson at P.O. Box 3077, Culver City, CA 90231.

153 Ideas for Totally No-Cost Marketing, by Pete Silver, provides brief creative ideas and practical tips about attracting and retaining customers and reducing the time you need to market your product or service. It covers the bases and is a checklist that emerged from Silver's extensive experience leading marketing seminars. The booklet costs five dollars and is available from the Marketing Communications Report, P.O. Box 2152, South Miami, FL 33243-2152.

Magazines

MacHome Journal simplifies computer use for the home-based Macintosh user and is free of technical jargon. Lively writing and elegant design distinguish this monthly magazine. One year: $19.95. *MacHome Journal,* P.O. Box 469, Mt. Morris, IL 61054. (800) 800-6542.

Entrepreneur, available on most newsstands, is the oldest and most respected magazine devoted to entrepreneurship. It features profiles of successful entrepreneurs and articles about motivation, venture capital, taxation, franchising, and how to analyze the weaknesses in your business. One year: $19.97. *Entrepreneur,* P.O. Box 50368, Boulder, CO 80321-0368.

Home Office Computing is a widely read monthly that focuses on small home-based businesses and how technology empowers them. It covers new products and includes technical articles, interesting interviews, and profiles. *Home Office Computing,* 730 Broadway, New York, NY 10003. (800) 866-5821. You can reach *Home Office Computing* on all the major online services.

Success, founded in 1909, is devoted to salesmanship, self-esteem, motivation, and entrepreneurship. Aimed at the corporate culture and the independent spirit, this lively magazine is published ten times a year and covers subjects ranging from education, franchising, and finance to sophisticated and futuristic ideas such as nanotechnology. One year: $14.97. *Success,* P.O. Box 3036, Harlan, IA 51593.

Working Woman describes itself accurately as "an intelligent, investigative, gutsy, sometimes irreverent, and fun magazine for professional women." Articles cover corporate life, small business, fashion, investment strategies, and success stories of women entrepreneurs. One year, $11.97. *Working Woman,* P.O. Box 3276, Harlan IA 51593-2456.

Newsletters

If you found this book useful, you might like to subscribe to *Success Working from Home,* a bimonthly newsletter I publish that delivers timely articles of fact and opinion from guest experts, plus stories about home-based businesses in the United States and Canada. One year: $36. Pro-rated refund guarantee. Jeff Berner, P.O. Box 244, Dept. BK, Dillon Beach, CA 94929.

At Work, a bimonthly newsletter, is a rich resource for people at all levels of management who want to achieve more congruence between their personal values and their working life. It supports those working to create more humane and effective organizations. One year: $75. Berrett-Koehler Publishers, Inc., 155 Montgomery Street, San Francisco, CA 94104-4109.

An excellent eight-page quarterly, *The Kern Report: Trends and Issues in Home-Based Business and Telecommuting,* edited by Coralee Kern, explores government policy issues as they affect home-based business, and the loneliness of the home-based worker. It also includes trends, profiles, and a wide range of resources. One year: $89. The Kern Report, P.O. Box 14850, Chicago, IL 60614. Fax, (312) 880-2409.

Home Business Line, the monthly newsletter from the American Home Business Association, is included in the association's seventy-five-dollar annual fee. A typical eight-page issue carries articles about whether or not to compute, how to work with independent contractors and small agencies, Keogh Plans, putting family members on the payroll, zoning, and networking. American Home Business Association, 397 Post Road, Darien, CT 06820.

Self-Employment Survival Letter, edited by Barbara Brabec, who has published this unpretentious twenty-eight-page quarterly for more than a decade. It is a patchwork of quaint anecdotes and useful tips and resources focusing on modest home-based businesses. One year: $29. Barbara Brabec, P.O. Box 2127, Naperville, IL 60567.

Bottom Line/Personal is a twice-monthly, sixteen-page newsletter designed to help those who are very busy with their careers handle their personal lives more effectively. Highly readable, it delivers concise information gathered from knowledgeable sources and is free of advertising. One year: $49. Boardroom Reports, Inc., 330 West 42d Street, New York, NY 10036.

Home-Based Business News is a bimonthly newsletter written for the new home business operator, providing news about taxes, marketing, consulting services, technology, and the law. One year: $15. Home-Based Business News, 0424 SW Pendleton, Portland, OR 97201. (503) 246-3452.

Print and Broadcast Resources of Broader Interest

Your Company is a quarterly publication sent at no charge to American Express Corporate Cardmembers and is available for four dollars per issue to others. This lively magazine has featured articles about a mother-daughter team that runs a custom auto accessories mail-order business, and a husband and wife who publish a newsletter for parents about their children's education. *Your Company,* American Express Publishing Corporation, 1120 Avenue of the Americas, New York, NY 10036.

Utne Reader, subtitled, "The best of the alternative press," is a bimonthly collection of articles ranging from alternative ways of making a living to ecology, censorship, healing arts, politics, and other subjects the mainstream press usually skims over or ignores. A consistently good read with a thought-provoking variety of subject matter, the magazine also helps its readers organize local "salons" for discussions with like-minded neighbors. One year: $18. *Utne Reader,* Subscriber Services, P.O. Box 1974, Marion, OH 43306-2074.

Export Today, founded in 1985 and free to qualified business people, covers such topics as "The 10 Most Overlooked Export Markets," "Mexico's Seven Best Sectors," "Ocean Carrier Niche Services," and "Asia: 5 New Markets in the Shadow of the Tigers." It includes the names and addresses of development banks, trade advocacy organizations, and international online services and databases devoted to business. Send your subscription query to: *Export Today Magazine,* 733 15th Street NW, Suite 1100, Washington, DC 20005.

The Whole Work Catalog is a good source of books devoted to the home office, self-employment, "green" careers, and alternative ways of making a living. It is distributed free by The New Careers Center, 1515-23d Street, P. O. Box 339-CT, Boulder, CO 80306.

Marketplace is an informative and entertaining radio program that covers a wide range of business and financial subjects. You will hear interviews with experts in self-employment, retirement planning, mergers, stocks, bonds, insurance, and international trade. You can hear it weekdays over most FM stations that carry National Public Radio.

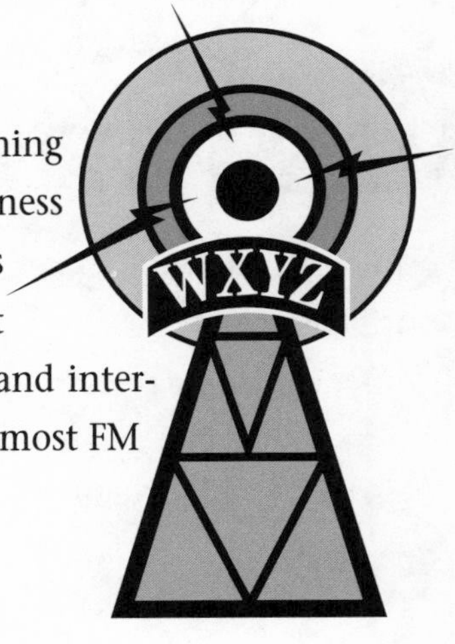

WXYZ

Government Publications and Services

The General Services Administration of the U.S. government publishes the "Consumer Information Catalog," which lists booklets about careers, federal programs, money management, securing business credit, and other topics. Participating federal agencies which offer booklets through this catalog include the Departments of Commerce, Defense, Energy, Interior, and State. Many of the booklets listed are free; others are sold at nominal cost. To get your copy, contact the Consumer Information Center, P.O. Box 100, Pueblo, CO 81002.

The Small Business Administration offers a series of inexpensive (one dollar or less) publications about starting and managing a home-based business. Order a free publications list by phoning the SBA Answer Line at (800) 827-5722. "Home Business," one of the booklets available from the SBA, is an extensive bibliography of information sources. It costs fifty cents per copy and can be ordered from the SBA at P.O. Box 30, Denver, CO 80201-0030.

The SBA also maintains Small Business Information Centers across the country. Each Business Information Center offers an electronic bulletin board, computer databases, online information exchange, periodicals and brochures, videotapes, reference material, start-up guides, applications software, computer tutorials, and interactive media. They also maintain an electronic bulletin board and offer electronic one-on-one counseling. The electronic bulletin board system is available twenty-four hours a day, seven days a week at (800) 859-4636 for 2400-baud modems and at (800) 697-4636 for 9600-baud modems.

Basic information and continually updated calendars of events listed by locale can be accessed on the SBA electronic bulletin board. Through SBA On-Line, another electronic bulletin board, anyone with a computer and modem can access a national calendar of events, which features such items as training programs, small-business seminars, international trade fairs, information on SBA loan programs and financial management services, and government assistance for small businesses. There are also programs to benefit women, minorities, and veterans. The SBA also has a loan program for small businesses that may otherwise be unable to secure capital.

The majority of SBA-sponsored training and counseling is conducted through its two largest resources, the Service Corps of Retired Executives (SCORE) and Small Business Development Centers (SBDCs). Both provide management assistance, training, and counseling to present and prospective small business owners.

SCORE is composed of retired business professionals nationwide who provide free counseling. SCORE conducts workshops on a variety of subjects, including how to start a new business, for a small fee. There are more than 750 SCORE locations nationwide, with 13,000 volunteer counselors representing many areas of expertise. You can make an appointment to confer with a SCORE counselor by phone or in person. Each SCORE office has its own local telephone directory listing.

The SBDC program provides counseling, training, and research assistance in all aspects of business management, including financial, marketing, production, organization, and technical problems. The centers are generally located on college and university campuses and are a cooperative effort among the educational community, private sector groups, and state, local, and federal government. There are 56 SBDCs in 49 states, the District of Columbia, Puerto Rico, and the Virgin Islands. There are more than 600 SBDC service locations nationwide.

CREDITS

Elephant Enterprises brochure on page 67 by C.G. Walker

Illustrations/trademarks on pages 5, 15, 37, 53, 54, 113, 119 are reprinted with permission of Eric Baker. *Trademarks of the '20s and 30's*, Eric Baker and Tyler Blik, Chronicle Books, 1985

Illustrations on pages 8, 19, 22, 24, 44, 60, 95, 131, 139, 149 by Wanda J. Hale

Illustration on page 13 by Robert Gumpertz

Images on pages 39, 69, 79, 83, 93, 96, 97, 102, 118, 128 are from the Jeff Berner Archive

Postage stamps on pages 16, 26, 76, 77, 100 are from the Jeff Berner Archive

Photograph *Big Sur, 1967* on page 134 by the author

Photographs on pages 81, 82, 104 by Glen Matsumura

Spectrum business card/logo and ad design on pages 63, 85 by Wanda J. Hale

Spiffy logo on page 64 by Wanda Hale

Spoke Folk business card/logo on page 65 by C.G. Walker & Michael Quillman

The Lazy JB Ranch (1989), miniature diorama (6'L, 3'W, 15"H), on page 101 by the author. Courtesy The Museum of Miniatures, Los Angeles

Wrist Sundial on page 43 by Fossil. Photograph by C.G.Walker

Front cover photo illustration by Jeff Berner and Walker & Hale. Photographed in author's home office.

Back Cover photo of the Author by Vera, Mill Valley, CA

INDEX

D

E

F

G

H

I

Q

R

S

T

ABOUT THE AUTHOR

Jeff Berner has combined the worlds of writing, teaching, art, and technology for the past thirty years. He is a former *San Francisco Chronicle* columnist, and is the author of eleven books including *At Your Fingertips: Making the Most of the Micro,* the companion volume to the BBC/PBS-TV series.

In 1968 he founded The Innerspace Project, an interdisciplinary think-tank and management firm consulting to major American and Canadian companies. In the mid-1980s he launched The Clarity Group, devoted to the writing and design of plain-language user guides for expert system-building shells, decision support software, and desktop publishing packages.

His photographic books include *The Photographic Experience* and *The Foolproof Guide to Taking Pictures,* and his work has received two awards from *Life* magazine, and the DESI:GRAPHICS:USA Award for photography and book design for *Uncarved Block, Unbleached Silk: The Mystery of Life,* by the late Alan Watts. His photography appears in textbooks, annual reports, and magazines such as *Psychology Today* and *Omni.*

Jeff Berner teaches "Awakening Vision Through Conscious Photography" workshops at Esalen Institute, Big Sur California, where he also conducts "The Joy of Working from Home: Making a Life while Making a Living" seminars.

As Extension Instructor in French Culture, he created and taught avant-garde art history courses at the University of California, Berkeley and San Francisco Centers; at The San Francisco Art Institute, and elsewhere.

He has been an active member of the international conceptual/performance art movement, Fluxus, since 1966, and his own art documentation collection, "Aktual Art International," has been shown at the San Francisco Museum of Modern Art and at the Stanford University Art Gallery. In recent years, Mr. Berner has been building 1/12th scale miniature dioramas, the first of which is "The Lazy JB Ranch," on display at the Museum of Miniatures, Los Angeles.